By What
Authority
Do We
Teach?

Other Works by Robert W. Pazmiño
Foundational Issues in Christian Education
*Latin American Journey: Insights for Christian Education
in North America*
Principles and Practices of Christian Education
The Seminary in the City

By What Authority Do We Teach?

Sources for Empowering Christian Educators

Robert W. Pazmiño

 **Baker Books**

A Division of Baker Book House Co
Grand Rapids, Michigan 49516

Published by Baker Books,
a division of Baker Book House Company
P.O. Box 6287
Grand Rapids, Michigan 49516-6287

Printed in the United States of America

Library of Congress Cataloging-in-Publication Data

Pazmiño, Robert W., 1948–
    By what authority do we teach? : sources for empowering
Christian educators / Robert W. Pazmiño.
        p.   cm.
    Includes bibliographical references and index.
    ISBN 0-8010-7129-1
    1. Christian education—Philosophy. 2. Teaching—religious
aspects—Christianity. 3. Authority (Religion) I. Title.
BV1464.P379   1994
268'.001—dc20   94-1704

Scripture references are from the New Revised Standard Version of the Bible.

To
My students and colleagues in theological education

Contents

Introduction

The Gospel of Luke describes an encounter that Jesus had with the chief priests and the teachers of the law in the temple courts at Jerusalem (20:1–8). On that occasion Jesus is asked two questions: By what authority are you doing these things? and Who gave you this authority? The response recorded by the writer of Luke is noteworthy. Jesus did not answer the questions, but instead posed a question for the priests and the teachers themselves to consider: By what authority did John the Baptist do the things he did? John had been baptizing persons in the Jordan River, and Jesus wanted to know if those who questioned him believed that this baptism came from heaven or was of human origin. In other words, was John's authority of a divine source or merely human and therefore questionable?

When the priests and the teachers declined to answer Jesus' question, he refused to respond to their inquiry regarding his authority. Jesus' question served to reveal the intent of their questions along with their commitments to respond to God as discerned through their view of the words of God's prophet, John the Baptist. The priests and the teachers knew that a direct response to Jesus' question would reveal either their lack of belief in God or their refusal to recognize popular perceptions of a prophet's authority. Their response—denying knowledge of John's authority—was the safe alternative to self-disclosure and the perceived risk of death by stoning. Yet for all their scheming, these religious leaders had asked the right question. They recognized a critical issue that affects every ministry, namely, the authority underlying it.

This work serves to confront the question posed for Jesus in relation to the basis of authority for teaching. It does not opt for the lack of response of the priests and the teachers as they were questioned about the authority of John the Baptist. Risks are inherent in any answer and in any work such as this text, but they are unavoidable in responding to the challenge posed for the church of Jesus Christ in an age that systematically questions authority. The emergence of a "hermeneutics of suspicion," a questioning of the interests and motives of those who interpret authoritatively, is warranted in the light of the historical abuse of authority and the corresponding decline of leadership in all areas of personal and corporate life. This abuse and decline has been particularly apparent over the past several years through press accounts that disclose the wrongdoing of leaders in all areas of public life. Despite the real problems that exist with the use and abuse of authority, a consideration of authority is essential for religious faith in general and for the Christian faith in particular.

P. T. Forsyth (1848–1921), a preacher and theologian whose insights were prophetic, observed:

> The principle of authority is ultimately the whole religious question, that an authority of any practical kind draws its meaning and its right only from the soul's relation to its God, that this is so not only for religion strictly so called, nor for a Church, but for public life, social life, and the whole history and career of humanity. . . . The one practical authority for human society is the God who in Christ comes in such judging and redeeming action that we are no more our own at all.[1]

The question of authority has particular practical importance in the ministries of Christian education with the need to pass on to future generations a true and reliable word. Children, youth, and adults have every right to ask questions about the authority of those who serve as their teachers and mentors. But posing questions does not dismiss the need to heed that which is, in fact, authoritative. The unwillingness to respond to legitimate moral

1. P. T. Forsyth, *The Principle of Authority in Relation to Certainty, Sanctity and Society: An Essay in the Philosophy of Experimental Religion*, 2d ed. (London: Independent, 1952), 2-4.

and spiritual authority is a characteristic of humanity that the Scriptures define as "sin," and sin is manifested in a wide variety of responses to both divine and human authority. Some responses to authority represent a creative but questionable avoidance of responsibility and accountability in life. This work raises the question of authority in the hope of fostering a faithful response to God and others in both the thought and the practice of Christian education.

Chapter 1, drawing upon Scripture (the primary source for theological authority) explores the question of God's authority; Forsyth described God as the "fontal authority," the ultimate source of authority in life.[2] The chapter proposes a trinitarian model of authority: God the Creator or Father, the Redeemer or Son Jesus Christ, and the Holy Spirit, our Sustainer. It also defines believers' authority as it relates to God's call to teach in the faith community.

Teaching is a representative ministry in the faith community, and the church must be open to God's continuing work of transformation in this ministry. Chapter 2 discusses the church as the context for authoritative teaching and as a secondary source for theological authority. Ecclesiastical authority that draws upon the Scriptures along with the insights gained from church traditions is exercised within the community.

Chapter 3 develops the concept of teaching as a gift of the Holy Spirit to persons who are to exercise that gift within the church and for its advancement.

The place of personal experience is considered in chapter 4, along with the issue of praxis in teaching. Experience with God and within the world provides a third element for theological authority.

Chapter 5 explores the place of expertise, study, and reason in teaching and the access that teachers provide to various communities of discourse and wisdom. Experience in teaching is intellectual and makes use of reason and study. Such reason and study result in expertise that is shared with others through teaching.

The final chapter, 6, wrestles with the authority of truth in an age of pluralism, especially in light of the call for contextualiza-

2. Ibid.

tion in a religiously and culturally diverse world. How can Christians relate to a religiously pluralistic world while maintaining their identity?

I wish to thank three faculty colleagues at Andover Newton Theological School for initiating my thoughts regarding questions about authority in teaching. In the summer of 1987 Gabriel Fackre, Jean and Daniel Novotny, and I provided leadership at a continuing education conference at the Craigville Conference Center on Cape Cod, Massachusetts. The theme of that conference was "Authority in the Church." Working with these seasoned colleagues planted the seeds and inspiration for this work.

This work is the third text in a theological trilogy for Christian education, all published by Baker Book House. I want to thank Allan Fisher of Baker for his willingness to support a new voice in the field of Christian education in 1986. My first work, *Foundational Issues in Christian Education*, explored the biblical, theological, philosophical, historical, sociological, psychological, and curricular foundations of Christian education.[3] The sequel to that work, *Principles and Practices of Christian Education*, outlined principles and guidelines for the practice of Christian education.[4] It drew upon a distinctly evangelical theological stance in formulating an approach or model and in identifying two underlying forms and two complementary principles. This third volume, *By What Authority Do We Teach?*, addresses a foundational theological question of our time, the question of authority as it relates to Christian education. Although it draws upon an evangelical theology, it strives to maintain an ecumenical commitment. It therefore readily draws upon ecumenical sources to challenge evangelical readers as they contribute to the wider theological dialogue. Openness to this wider dialogue provides opportunity to understand the distinctives of one's theological identity.

I want to also thank those who provided feedback on various drafts of this work: Gabriel Fackre, who held my feet to the theo-

---

3. Robert W. Pazmiño, *Foundational Issues in Christian Education: An Introduction in Evangelical Perspective* (Grand Rapids: Baker, 1988).
4. Robert W. Pazmiño, *Principles and Practices of Christian Education: An Evangelical Perspective* (Grand Rapids: Baker, 1992).

logical fires; a teaching assistant, Linda Reynolds, who raised practical implications from her teaching experience; and my colleagues in the field, Julie Gorman, Ronald Habermas, Kevin Lawson, and Eileen Starr. Their comments helped to refine my thoughts and their presentation in this text.

1

Authority of God and God's Call

Before they explore the question of authority in relation to God, persons who teach must consider the preliminary matter of definition. What is meant by authority? As Hannah Arendt observed, in Western civilization the concept of authority derives from the Roman idea that those in authority constantly augment the foundation of the ancestors or the founders of Rome. This assumes that one can name the foundations of the ancestors or the founders and that the foundations merit continuation. In this sense, the term *authority* derives from the Latin verb *augere* (to augment) and the noun *auctoritas* (authority itself).[1] Augmentation implies points of continuity with what has occurred in the past. But in a societal context of rapid or revolutionary change the points of continuity may be difficult to discern. In

1. Hannah Arendt, *Between Past and Future: Eight Exercises in Political Thought* (New York: Viking, 1968), 120–28.

15

such a situation, past authorities are not viewed as reliable and people search for new authorities to guide their lives. This is the case in a postmodern age.[2]

Building upon the Latin noun *auctoritas*, the English word *author* denotes that one is an authority and can therefore speak or write reliably on certain matters. An author is ideally one who explores the past of the ancestors as well as the challenges of the present and future.[3] From their search, authors offer new or renewed perspectives that serve as guides or authorities for others. An author seeks to imaginatively build upon the prior works of others and yet to speak with a distinct and an authoritative voice. This is an assumption of the author of any book, including the one you are now reading. But questions must be posed for authors in relation to their authority and the truth they seek to disclose.

Active reading of this and any written work assumes that readers are posing questions if they are to critically appropriate and apply the writing. Being in print does not assure the legitimacy of what any author shares with his or her readers. An appeal to higher authorities or at least a comparison with other authorities not only is warranted but also is required for the discernment of the truth. The author of this work invites readers to such an active and critical reading with the hope that some light might be shed on the foundational question of authority.

In the Christian tradition, God is viewed as the author of life and faith, the fontal authority. We therefore rely upon God, who provides the foundation or the grounding for understanding authority. In the Christian tradition the Scriptures have been the primary source for understanding God. The Scriptures are the source for Christian truth and serve as the essential foundation for addressing the question of authority. Scriptures serve as the "mediate authority" for Christian faith and life in the sense that they mediate God's revelation in Jesus Christ, the one mediator between God and humankind.[4]

2. Note Gabriel Moran's discussion of postmodernity in "Response to William Kennedy," *Religious Education* (Fall 1992): 515.

3. Letty M. Russell, "Authority in Mutual Ministry," *Quarterly Review* 6 (Spring 1986): 11.

4. See Dennis Campbell, *Authority and the Renewal of American Theology* (Philadelphia: United Church Press, 1976), 2ff.

Authority in the Scriptures

In the New Testament "authority" is the English translation for the Greek term *exousia*. *Exousia* has a variety of meanings, including four identified here. Each of the four distinct meanings—*possession, person, place, precedent*—provides insights. First, authority can refer to possession or use of power.[5] The lives, actions, and words of persons give evidence of possession and use of power. In relation to teaching the question is Whose words are heeded and whose lives and actions are modeled? Those who have such an influence possess and exercise authority explicitly or implicitly in the life of a community.

Second, authority can refer to a person and his or her legal or moral right to exercise power.[6] In relation to teaching the question posed is Who has the right and obligation to teach? In general, Christians have responded to this question by naming parents, teachers, pastors, and various leaders in the faith community as well as in public life. But in a real sense all Christian persons can serve as teachers in the areas of their ministry. In this sense teaching is defined broadly.

Third, authority can refer to the place, the domain or the dominion within which power is exercised.[7] Parents exercise authority in the home; pastors exercise authority in the church and the community; and teachers exercise authority in the classroom and the school environment. The description of distinct domains may suggest that conflicts do not exist at the interface of these domains, but conflicts emerge along with points of confirmation and complementarity of the lessons taught by different authorities. The negotiation of these conflicts is a primary task for the Christian church and is a subject for study in Christian education. Which authorities have priority in what situation and why?

Fourth, authority can refer to the precedent appealed to in support of an action or an opinion, the appeal to a higher power.[8]

5. John Marsh, "Authority," in *The Interpreter's Dictionary of the Bible*, ed. George A. Buttrick (Nashville: Abingdon, 1962), 319.
6. Ibid.
7. Ibid.
8. Ibid.

In a Christian world view the ultimate appeal is to God, the Father, Son, and Holy Spirit. All human authority is viewed as derived from God, the source, the fontal authority. The apostle Paul noted in his epistle to the Romans that "there is no authority except from God, and those authorities that exist have been instituted by God" (Rom. 13:1b). The danger in any discussion of authority is a rush to reconcile any conflict by a referral to God as the cosmic referee. That stance is not advocated in this work, but rather a serious wrestling with God's authority in all of life and the encounter of diverse human authorities as instituted by God. Those authorities include theological and ecclesiastical ones. As John Marsh observed, "The focus of biblical usage is in the authority which belongs to God alone, all other authority being subordinate and derivative."[9] Thus the starting point for any discussion of authority in the Christian community is God's authority.

The Definition of Authority

The definitions of authority in the four suggested scriptural meanings all refer to power. Therefore a key question to raise is What is the relationship of authority to power? Marsh suggests that "in the Bible, as in modern usage, authority is closely connected with power, though usually, but not always, distinguished from it."[10] Power or *dynamis* refers to the inherent capacity of someone or something to carry out a task or an activity, whether it be physical, as in getting up and walking; spiritual, as in being in communion with God; moral, as in standing for that which is just and right; military, as in defending a territory or defeating an enemy; political, as in legislating, executing, or judging public policies and laws; or economic, as in having capital to fund and sustain a business venture. Power can be defined as the ability to accomplish desired ends. It also can refer to a largely spontaneous expression of power, and its root simply means "to be able." Authority, in contrast with power, refers only to people in their communal and institutional settings, in the web of human need and

9. Ibid.
10. Ibid.

18

interdependence. Authority indicates the power to act that is given as a right to anyone by virtue of the position she or he holds. That position may be explicit or implicit in the life of a community. Authority denotes the power that persons display in the areas of legal, political, social, moral, or religious affairs. It is always linked with a particular relation, position, or mandate, and assumes one's responsibility, accountability, and integrity in exercising one's right.[11] Institutional authority within the Christian church is evaluated in relation to the theological authority that is exercised (see chap. 2).

Authority can therefore be defined as legitimate, recognized, and/or verifiable power that certain persons possess in various areas of life by virtue of their relationships with others. As Richard Sennet suggests, authority is a relational bond that leads persons to give assent without coercion because they find security in the real or imagined strength of others.[12] In relation to teaching, authority is the legitimate, recognized, and/or verifiable power of those persons recognized and functioning as teachers. But such teaching authority is vitally connected with the relational bond that exists between teachers and those persons being taught, and those in need of teaching for their life. Without the presence of students or disciples, the perceived or actual authority of teachers becomes a question divorced from reality and practice. Students or those who sit with teachers are to give assent or dissent to the content that teachers share.

As Sennet suggests, the assent of students to the content teachers share should flow without coercion; he discounts persuasion in his understanding of authority (a perspective with which this author differs). Coercion implies a lack of personal, rational, and intentional choice, and so is to be opposed. But persuasion, different from what Sennet indicates, assumes the presence of such a choice with the possibility of alternatives. My perspective assumes that conflict and choice are inevitable in the proper exercise of authority. A careful consideration of both coercion and

11. Christian Blendinger, "Might, Authority, Throne," in *The New International Dictionary of New Testament Theology*, ed. Colin Brown, 3 vols. (Grand Rapids: Zondervan, 1976), 2:600, 607.
12. Richard Sennet, *Authority* (New York: Vintage, 1981), 16–27.

persuasion is required today because of the history of abusing authority in all areas of community life.

The work of Robert Greenleaf is insightful in making some further distinctions in the use and abuse of authority and its persuasive power. *Influence in teaching can be contrasted with manipulation and persuasion can be contrasted with coercion.* Influence involves mutual knowledge and gives other persons freedom to disagree. With influence there is no imposition of truth or value. It allows others to make a decision. Manipulation is the exploitation, use, and/or control of other people who are viewed as objects or things. Manipulation involves deception and levels of unawareness on the part of those manipulated. Manipulation is guiding people into beliefs or actions that they do not fully understand.[13] Thus the proper exercise of authority in teaching would allow for influence, but its abuse would include manipulation. A similar comparison holds for persuasion and coercion.

Persuasion is the act of encouraging others to confirm the rightness of a belief or an action by their own intuition, conscious logic, and discernment. Coercion is the use, or threat of use, of covert or overt actions or penalties, the exploitation of weaknesses or sentiments, or any application of pressure to convince others.[14] Thus the proper exercise of authority affirms persuasion in teaching while avoiding coercion. This balance is best modeled in the example of God the Father's authority, in the teaching ministry of Jesus Christ, and in the work of the Holy Spirit to undergird the teaching of Christ and Christians today. These models deserve our careful attention as we consider theological reflections on the question of authority.

A Trinitarian Model

Nels Ferré, a systematic theologian, suggested that a theology for Christian education could consider God the Father as the

13. Robert K. Greenleaf, *Servant: Retrospect and Prospect* (Peterborough, N.H.: Center for Applied Studies and Windy Row Press, 1980), 22–23.
14. Ibid. See also Robert K. Greenleaf, *Teacher as Servant: A Parable* (Newton Centre, Mass.: Robert K. Greenleaf Center, 1987).

20

educator, Jesus Christ the Son as the exemplar, and the Holy Spirit as the tutor[15] (see fig. 1).

Figure 1
A Trinitarian Model

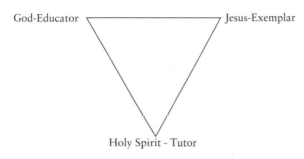

God-Educator ⟋⟍ Jesus-Exemplar

Holy Spirit - Tutor

God as the Creator is the educator from whom all the content of education issues. Jesus as the Exemplar or mentor is the model or master teacher who in his person exemplifies all that a teacher should be in his relationships with his disciples or students. The Holy Spirit as the Tutor is the counselor or community consultant who sustains the life of the Christian community and the wider society in ways that fulfill God's purposes. All three persons of the Trinity must be seen as working cooperatively and in concert. Ferré's theological foundation affirms a trinitarian model to guide the exploration of the question of authority within the Christian faith.

A Scripture passage (1 Cor. 12:4–6) also suggests a trinitarian model: "Now there are varieties of gifts, but the same Spirit; and there are varieties of services, but the same Lord; and there are varieties of activities, but it is the same God who activates all of them in everyone." Christians have received from the Holy Spirit varieties of spiritual gifts for teaching. They are to minister in the community and society, and doing so are to rely upon the refreshment, empowerment, and joy of the Spirit. Christians have also received varieties of services from their Lord in following the example of the master teacher, Jesus Christ. In their teaching service Christians are called to reflect in their persons and lives the love

15. Nels F. S. Ferré, *A Theology for Christian Education* (Philadelphia: Westminster, 1967).

21

of Christ for humankind. Varieties of activities fulfill God the Father's call and mission in the world. One such activity is sharing the content of God's revelation through teaching the Christian faith to current and future generations.

Ferré's trinitarian model identifies the foundations for authoritative teaching. Teaching itself can be defined as the process of sharing content with persons in the context of their community and society. That content includes cognitive, affective, and behavioral aspects, and in the case of Christian teaching fosters an intellectual, emotional, and active response to the gospel. For the task of teaching, Christians can explore the question of authority in relation to the authority of the three persons of the Trinity.

God's Authority

In the ancient world, authoritative teaching built upon the insights of a succession of teachers that reached back to the founders or the ancestors of a society. From a theistic perspective that succession originates with God, the author and builder of creation and all of life. God is viewed as the creator, sustainer, and sovereign of the universe and therefore the source of all authority. God is absolutely free to act in relation to the creation and its providential care. God's influence and persuasive presence is a reality throughout time and space, but is revealed most especially in Jesus Christ, the second person of the Trinity, in his incarnation. Humans are gifted with God's special revelation in discerning the nature of life and must choose to affirm or to deny that spiritual revelation while struggling to interpret it. Persons choose to recognize or to ignore God's authority in relation to their personal and corporate life, and their choices have inevitable consequences.

The apostle Paul, echoing Old Testament prophets, compared God with a potter who can do what one likes with the clay (Rom. 9:21; Isa. 29:16; 45:9; Jer. 18:6). God as creator can shape and mold the creation according to God's design. God's authority in this process is legitimate and just. But the paradox of God's exercise of authority is the way in which God allows for the exercise of human authority and freedom. God's authority serves to empower persons in their experience of abundant life that fulfills God's original designs for creation in an amazing way.

God's authority creates freedom for humanity. God's authority is the source for liberating power in human experience through the person and ministry of Jesus the Christ. The true authority of God is an authority for action in all of life. The living God's assertion of authority is appropriate because God has the right to guide all human action and history. God's authority is made most clear in the cross of Jesus Christ that calls for the human response of obedience.[16] Through obedience to God as revealed in Jesus Christ, persons find their true freedom and liberty that calls them into covenant and partnership.

God is the ultimate teacher or educator of humankind. God was at work instructing and restoring the life of creation and the covenant community from the time of the fall, and that work has continued throughout history. The insight of Job's rebuker, the young man Elihu, can be heeded: "See, God is exalted in his power; who is a teacher like him?" (Job 36:22). God's teaching transcends what human experience or reason can readily fathom, even in the midst of suffering and pain as Job experienced them.

God is active in guiding humanity and disclosing truth to those often viewed as least likely to possess the wisdom needed to address complex human problems. The apostle Paul reflected upon this reality (1 Corinthians 1:27-31):

> But God chose what is foolish in the world to shame the wise; God chose what is weak in the world to shame the strong; God chose what is low and despised in the world, things that are not, to reduce to nothing things that are, so that no one might boast in the presence of God. He is the source of your life in Jesus Christ, who became for us wisdom from God, and righteousness and sanctification and redemption, in order that, as it is written, "Let the one who boasts, boast in the Lord."

Paul's reflection serves to introduce the importance of Jesus for understanding the place of authority in teaching. Jesus is the fullest expression of God's revelation, and his use of authority is particularly instructive for Christian teachers.

16. These insights are shared by P. T. Forsyth, *The Principle of Authority in Relation to Certainty, Sanctity and Society: An Essay in the Philosophy of Experiential Religion* (London: Independence, 1952), 8–11.

Jesus' Authority

The self-revelation of God in Jesus Christ and through the continuing ministry of the Holy Spirit is the source of authority in the lives of Christians, those who follow Christ as disciples. In Jesus Christ there is a new disclosure of what divine authority is like. As the incarnate Son of God, Jesus taught with authority (Mark 1:22), not as the scribes did. Jesus' authority was not even as that of the prophets who declared, "Thus saith the Lord." Jesus started with a new locus of authority: "I say to you!" (Matt. 5:22, 28, 32, 34, 39, 44).

Jesus' authority in teaching provoked amazement or astonishment (Mark 1:22, 27; Matt. 7:28–29; Luke 4:32). The scribes were guided by their teaching tradition (Matt. 7:29), whereas Jesus, the anointed one, not only received his words from the mouth of God, as did Moses and the prophets, but also spoke with the authority of the one who uniquely knows and reveals God (Matt. 11:27; Luke 10:22; Matt. 28:18; John 3:35; 13:3; 10:15; 17:25).

In John's Gospel Jesus's plenipotentiary (with full potential) authority is based on the fact that he is God's only begotten Son and that he is sent on a specific mission (John 17:2). Jesus is granted authority over all persons. He has also been given the authority to judge at the end of time (John 5:27). But with this authority Jesus sought to save persons rather than to judge them in his earthly ministry (John 3:17–21). His power is not forcible domination, but freedom to be a servant to the world. He has the *exousia* to give his life and to take it up again (John 10:18). Jesus' sacrifice opens the way for believers to come to God (John 3:16; 14:6). Those who receive Jesus and believe in his name are given *exousia*, authority to become the children of God (John 1:12).

A plenipotentiary role carries full representative authority and responsibility. As the second person of the Trinity, Jesus exercised this role. While participating in a Tavistock conference weekend a number of years ago, I gained a new appreciation of the nature of a plenipotentiary role. (This conference developed from the work of Dr. A. K. Rice at the Center for Applied Social Research of the Tavistock Institute of Human Relations in London.) During the weekend, various roles in the life of small

24

groups are experientially explored. The roles include observer, delegate, and plenipotentiary. The distinction of these roles served to highlight the uniqueness of a plenipotentiary role.

An observer can only see and report on what happens to other groups' members in activities to which one is sent. A delegate carries messages and can enter discussion regarding those messages, but is not authorized to go beyond the directions of the sending group. But a plenipotentiary has full authority and responsibility in serving as a spokesperson for the sending group; he or she has binding power for all decisions made. I recall hedging and hesitating in assuming such responsibility for my group, although I had strongly advocated having this authority to negotiate with other groups. It was an awesome responsibility and I actively sought clarity from my sending small group before venturing out to interact with other groups.

In contrast with my reluctance and great hesitancy, Jesus assumed the full responsibilities of his sending group, namely, the Trinity itself. Jesus fully represented the godhead in his earthly ministry and exercised an authority that uniquely disclosed God. In this plenipotentiary role, Jesus was able to fulfill the purposes of God for the salvation of humankind and all creation. Therefore in his teaching a distinct authority was incarnated that called for the response of his hearers. Such a response resulted in either life or death as Jesus' hearers had to make a choice.

The choice of life offered in the gospel of Jesus Christ is foundational for exploring authority. P. T. Forsyth noted that if the gospel of Christ's grace is the only authority for fallen humanity, the seat of that authority is the Bible, and the witness is the faithful church.[17] Gabriel Fackre states this foundation for authority differently. He sees the Bible as the source of authority of which Christ is the center and for which the gospel is the substance.[18] It is crucial for Christian teachers to discern their relationship with Jesus Christ and the new life offered in his gospel. This discernment provides a ground, a foundation for their teaching.

17. P. T. Forsyth, *The Gospel and Authority: A P. T. Forsyth Reader*, ed. Marvin W. Anderson (Minneapolis: Augsburg, 1971), 41–42.
18. Gabriel Fackre, *The Christian Story: A Pastoral Systematics*, vol. 2, *Authority: Scripture in the Church for the World* (Grand Rapids: Eerdmans, 1987), 52.

It is important to note that the authority or *exousia* is not attributed to the gift or work of the Spirit in the teaching ministry of Jesus Christ. Whereas Jesus' power (*dynamis*) has its foundation in his being anointed by the Holy Spirit, his *exousia* is founded in his being sent as the preincarnate Son of God, the Lamb slain before the foundation of the world (Rev. 13:8). Thus his position in relation to God and the mandate for his ministry of redemption and reconciliation undergird his authority. His authority derives from his nature as God and his relation to God the Father. The impact of his teaching confirms Jesus' claim to have been sent by his Father. The distinction between authority and power is sustained in understanding Jesus' teaching authority. Furthermore, Jesus' ministry was persuasive, not coercive. In Mark 6:1–6, when Christ returned to his hometown, he wanted more than anything to convince his extended and communal family to believe in him and his mission. Yet, many rejected his claims. The writer records that the Son of God could perform only a few miracles because of their unbelief. Jesus refused to coerce others, although he had the power to do so. More than his desire to have them believe him, Jesus valued the freedom of individual choice.

A question for consideration is How does the distinction between power and authority relate to the teaching of Christians today? In what sense are Christians sent or called to teach and by whom are they sent? How can Christians be empowered to act upon the authority they have received in becoming children of God and disciples of Jesus Christ? A consideration of the Holy Spirit, the third person of the Trinity, and the Spirit's authority can assist us in addressing these questions.

The Holy Spirit's Authority

Jesus gave his disciples assurance of empowerment and enablement in his word at his ascension: "But you will receive power when the Holy Spirit has come upon you" (Acts 1:8). This is also the message in the words recorded in John 16:13: "When the Spirit of truth comes, he will guide you into all the truth." With the departure of the master teacher from earth, his disciples can rely upon the Holy Spirit to guide and to direct their ministries. The Holy Spirit is present at the birthing of the Christian church on the day of Pentecost (Acts 2:1–13) and is prominent in the accounts of the early church throughout the Book of Acts. The Holy Spirit was and is present to undergird the efforts of the church to teach and to speak with authority. The Holy Spirit works to sustain, nurture, probe, and challenge the Christian church in ways that accomplish Christ's agenda for the world. The Holy Spirit testifies of Christ and inspired the writers of the Scriptures. The Holy Spirit illumines the hearts and minds of those who seek to understand, live by, and teach the Scriptures. This agenda takes shape in relation to the values and perspectives of Christ's reign or realm, traditionally named as the kingdom of God. The authority of the Spirit is actively expressed in accomplishing God's mission in the world and in sustaining the active partnership of believers in that mission.

The authority of the Holy Spirit in teaching can be explored in relation to the authoritative Word of God. The Word of God is creative, living, and written. The creative Word is described in both Genesis 1 and John 1, where God is revealed in creation. As the Spirit of God sweeps over the face of the waters, as God speaks, all things are created. As the Spirit of God moves over the assembled disciples of Jesus, the Christian church is created (Acts 2). The creative Word is still active in the world, disclosing God and creating new possibilities as persons respond to God's calling to teach and to wrestle with both special and general revelation. The creative Word's ministry is in relation to the context of authoritative teaching in the gathered faith community and in the wider society and world.

The living Word encounters persons through the active presence and ministry of the Holy Spirit. The living Word is a person and the living Word's ministry is in relation to the persons engaged in authoritative teaching, namely, those called as teachers and those called as students. Forsyth observed that as persons our great authority must be a person, a person who is an active source of life, a person who is gathered up and consummated in a creative, redemptive act.[19] That person is Jesus the Christ who died upon the cross and was resurrected the third day. The Holy Spirit

19. Forsyth, *Principle of Authority*, 13.

27

is identified as the Spirit of Christ who makes available to humankind the surpassing grace of the crucified one in whom grace and truth have come (John 1:16).

The written Word is the essential source for authoritative teaching, and in relation to that teaching the written Word provides the basic content. The work of the Holy Spirit is in the inspiration of the texts of Scripture and in the illumination of those who seek to teach them or to be taught by them. The written Word provides the foundational, but not the exhaustive, content for authoritative teaching in the Christian faith. The particular danger for conservative Christians in relation to the written Word is to take the extreme view that the written Word is the believers' exhaustive authority. Such a view leads to biblicism, a view that the writers of Scripture did not take. Donald G. Bloesch provides a helpful perspective on biblicism, which he defines as

> viewing the Bible as an authority in and of itself. The dogmatic norm of the Reformers was not the Bible as such but rather the Word of God given in the Bible by the Spirit. . . . We need to recover the paradox that the Bible is both the infallible Word of God and the words of finite and sinful men who were, however, guided by the Spirit of God. We need to understand the Bible not as a document that can be proved or disproved, but as a sacrament, a veritable means of grace.[20]

With the written Word Christians have an authoritative source that requires careful and discerning interpretation. Such interpretation requires openness to the continuing ministry of the Holy Spirit as "ever new light and truth breaks forth from God's Holy Word."[21] As Forsyth noted, the Bible is the element that mediates the one great sacrament—the historic grace of God in Christ.[22] Therefore the Scriptures serve as the primary mediate authority.

The Holy Spirit is active in equipping and empowering Christians for their diverse ministries. A current interest in spirituality and spiritual formation from a Christian perspective is scandal-

20. Donald G. Bloesch, *The Crisis of Piety: Essays Toward a Theology of the Christian Life* (Colorado Springs: Helmers and Howard, 1988), 13–14.

21. Gabriel Fackre, *The Christian Story: A Narrative Interpretation of Basic Christian Doctrine*, rev. ed. (Grand Rapids: Eerdmans, 1984), 23.

22. Forsyth, *Gospel and Authority*, 46.

28

ized without being centered upon the person and work of the Holy Spirit. One's authority in teaching is intimately related to being called, gifted, empowered, and filled by the Holy Spirit. This assumes that Christians make available to the Holy Spirit their natural gifts and abilities. All of these gifts and abilities are gifts from God and find their highest fulfillment in service to God and in response to human need. The validation of the Spirit's authority in a teaching ministry is interpreted differently in distinct church traditions (see chap. 2). But common to all these traditions is the need for anointed teaching undergirded by the authority of the Holy Spirit to bring God's Word to bear on life today. This need requires that Christians discern their authority as believers responding to the call of God.

A challenge is posed for believers in discerning the promptings of the Spirit of truth for current and future ministries. This is more than just reading the times and affairs of human activities and sensing the ebb and flow of history in offering seasonal insights. A deep commitment and yearning for God's will and purposes is required of Christians, as is a willingness to wait upon God. This waiting necessitates discipline and often a sabbath time and space away from the routine preoccupations of life. Such waiting suggests that the Holy Spirit is also encountered in the commonplace affairs of life if believers are vulnerable and available. Availability implies a willingness to embrace one's authority and to act upon it as a gift to believers that is required for their service. It must be recognized with the current interest in diverse spiritualities that the person and work of the Holy Spirit cannot be separated from the ministry and purposes of Jesus Christ. *A claim to truth revealed by the Spirit must be tested by the Spirit of Christ as revealed in Scripture.* The hunger for spiritual teaching is met by authoritative teaching as guided by the Holy Spirit.

Believers' Authority

Marsh maintains that the relationships of human authorities to divine authority is articulated in the mutual relationships of king, prophet, priest, and judge found in the Scriptures. He suggests that together these relationships embodied the divine provision for authority in human life. Kings must rule in righteousness;

judges must deal justly; priests must make due expiation for sin; and the watchperson over all was the prophet, bound to no earthly master, servant only to God, speaking with divine authority the judgments of God on the faith community and the wider society alike.[23] By way of biblical illustration, David's sin with Bathsheba required the prophetic intervention of Nathan to maintain national life. Had Nathan failed, extensive corruption would have resulted within Israel's government. By way of modern application, similar gifted men and women, having complementary gifts in leadership, must guide and evaluate Christian institutions and organizations to avoid cycles of corruption and injustice. Thus a web of authorities exists that is ordained and ordered by God to provide stability in human corporate and personal life. That web also holds the potential of abuse if God's purposes are not fulfilled. Reference to the model of Jesus helps to discern the proper use of authority while avoiding its abuse.

Guillermo Cook, a missiologist, has observed that Jesus Christ has redefined the roles of king, priest, and prophet as they were modeled in the Old Testament. The royal or political mission of the king is redefined by Christ in terms of service to God, humanity, and the entire creation. The priestly mission is redefined by Christ in terms of sacrificial love, which might also be conceived in terms of steadfast love (Hosea 6:6). The prophetic mission is redefined by Christ in terms of incarnation, living out God's values in the world.[24] The mission of the judge in a final sense awaits the consummation and Christ's return, but is redefined in terms of Christ's advocacy for those on the margins of society and the call for peace with justice.

In the New Testament the decisive authoritative event is the resurrection of Jesus Christ. Christ has been raised "far above all rule and authority and power and dominion" (Eph. 1:21). From this position, Christ gave and gives authority to his followers in order to accomplish a fivefold mission. Followers have authority to forgive sins (John 20:23; Matt. 16:19; 18:18), heal diseases (Luke 9:1), expel demons (Mark 6:7), proclaim the coming of the

23. Marsh, "Authority," 319.
24. Guillermo Cook, *The Expectation of the Poor: Latin American Base Ecclesial Communities in Protestant Perspective* (Maryknoll, N.Y.: Orbis, 1985), 238.

kingdom (Matt. 10:7–8), and teach (Matt. 28:18–20). This mission can be summarized as the ministries of healing, preaching, and teaching.

The authority of believers (John 1:12) is founded in Christ. This authority implies both freedom and service. Martin Luther, in "The Freedom of a Christian," suggested that a Christian is [a] perfectly free [lord] of all, subject to none; a Christian is a perfectly dutiful servant of all, subject to all. This presents a paradox in terms of the exercise of authority, but a challenge for living the Christian life. The Christian is free to serve, sacrifice, and incarnate the love of God. The Christian has the authority to live this way from the commission of her or his resurrected Lord and Savior. Thus, our authority as Christians implies that we are free to serve, to care, and to be companions to others. The exalted Jesus Christ sends out disciples and empowers them for their service in the gospel (Matt. 28:18–20). Because Jesus possesses all authority in heaven and on earth, believers are assured of being sustained in their distinct callings or ministries and of being comforted by his presence forever. One such calling is the call to teach, the call to make disciples (Matt. 28:18–20). Teaching must be seen as a crucial ministry for Christians in every age in order to sustain the vitality of the faith community.

Judith Ruhe Diehl quotes Elton Trueblood: "If you are a Christian, you are a minister. . . . A non-ministering Christian is a contradiction in terms." It is important to note that in Latin *minister* refers to a servant or a minor, not a male cleric.[25] This fact has implications for the specific teaching ministry of women as well as men. Believers in Jesus Christ are called to be servants in all areas of human endeavor and are called to represent Christ through their words and deeds. The faithful exercise of their calling serves to either confirm or deny the authority given to them through their relationship with Jesus Christ. This perspective can be affirmed, but where is the rub for Christians today in relation to the exercise of their authority?

Christians, as ministers, may have trouble in accepting that we have authority and power today; and to reject power and its

25. Judith Ruhe Diehl, *A Woman's Place: Equal Partnership in Daily Ministry* (Philadelphia: Fortress, 1985), 83, quoting Elton Trueblood, "You Are a Minister" (pamphlet).

legitimate use is ultimately to reject God's gift and intention for Christians as we live in the world. To reject authority is to reject our position in Christ and our mandate or calling from Christ to be in relationship with God and others. That mandate is embodied in the two great commandments: loving God with all of our heart, soul, mind, and strength and loving our neighbors as ourselves. To reject our own and/or another's power and authority is to reject the responsibility and accountability implied in the recognition of this power and authority. Authority requires commitment. We are fearful of freedom, service, commitment, responsibility, accountability, authority, and power. This is in part justifiable, given the abuses of power and authority evident with others and ourselves. But the perfect love of God is able to cast out a fear that limits our service and to empower our ministries in freedom and joy (1 John 4:18). Ministry, teaching, and life are risky. To accept power and authority in the call of Christ to all his disciples and ministers is to accept that risk and to be free to serve. Beyond these personal and internal dimensions of appropriating authority, the corporate and external dimensions of authority operate.

In the United States we live in a society that regularly and systematically questions authority. This questioning relates to the cultural and social location of those who seek to interpret life and the Christian faith. Donald Guthrie, in considering the teaching of Jesus, raised an important question: Is the approach of Jesus' authoritative teaching relevant as a pattern for the present? He states, "The crux of the matter lies in the attitude toward authority." In Jesus' time the authority of elders and teachers was generally respected. In our age, traditional authorities have been widely overthrown. These facts, however, cannot be used to assume that the approach of Jesus is obsolete. "The modern rejection of authority is due to a lack of respect for its source, rather than a rejection of authority itself. . . . Truth carries its own authority."[26] In the case of Jesus, the source of authority is both valid and reliable. Jesus disclosed and incarnated truth (John 14:6) and promised to send the Spirit, who enables the disciples

26. Donald Guthrie, "Jesus," in *A History of Religious Educators*, ed. Elmer L. Towns (Grand Rapids: Baker, 1975), 37.

of Jesus to discern the truth (John 16:13). That same Spirit is available to believers today in their diverse ministries, including teaching.

In relation to our authority, we must ask ourselves if our lives model an integrity as was the case with Jesus. Is there an integration of what we claim or profess and what we live? We all deal with contradictions, sins, and shortcomings, but the verification of our call and authority is in part found in the fruits of our lives as it was evidenced in the life and ministry of our Lord Jesus Christ. The undergirding of any authority we claim or strive to embody is dependent upon our connection to the living tradition of Jesus Christ in our time, our connection to the gospel. This is not so distinct from what was the case in the ancient world.

In the New Testament world, authoritative teaching was demonstrated by showing a succession of teachers, a living tradition that was traced from the triune God, to the incarnate Christ in the person of Jesus, to the twelve apostles, to the teachers in the early church. This succession is made clear in Matthew 9:35–11:1, which explicitly addresses Jesus' instruction to the twelve apostles. The writer of Matthew describes Jesus as having completed a tour of towns and villages performing the three essential tasks of teaching, preaching and healing (Matt. 9:35). But Jesus had reached a point in his ministry where he could no longer do the work alone. It was the "time of the harvest" and workers were needed (Matt. 9:37–38). In this situation Jesus handed over to his disciples each of the three powers manifested in his personal ministry. The disciples had authority to heal (10:1), to preach (10:7), and to teach (28:18–20). They were called by, commissioned by, and made accountable to Jesus. The writer of Matthew assures his readers of a continuing responsibility and enablement for those who embrace the heritage of Jesus.

An Old Testament parallel of this succession of power is the story of Jacob and his twelve sons. At the end of Jacob's life a new era was to begin. Jacob had to hand over his mission and power to his sons (Gen. 48–49). Jacob's last testament involves passing on the mantle of authority to his descendants, just as Moses later did with Joshua, his successor (Deut. 31–34). In Matthew's Gospel account the harvest had come, Jesus' death was near, and the question of continuing leadership and responsibility was pre-

33

sented. The new era of the church was about to begin and the question of continuity in mission was essential. Jesus had to hand over his work to the Twelve if it was ever to continue. The transfer of authentic and authoritative teaching had a central place not only in the Gospel of Matthew, but also throughout the New Testament. The call and the authority passed on to the disciples served to transmit and to guard the tradition, not to control it. Control would limit the new light and truth that emerges from God's revelation in Scripture and the essential work of the Holy Spirit who was promised to the disciples.

For the writer of Matthew, Jesus' example was the highest form of teaching: "A disciple is not above the teacher, nor a slave above the master; it is enough for the disciple to be like the teacher" (Matt. 10:24–25a). Moreover, doing and teaching are linked (Matt. 7:24–27) with Jesus' disciples' call to live by his commandments and to teach others to do the same (Matt. 5:19). Being like Jesus and doing what he commanded provided for his first disciples (and provides for present-day disciples) the basis upon which to teach others. Jesus' recorded parting challenge to his disciples is to make disciples of others and to teach them to obey everything that he commanded them to be and to do (Matt. 28:18–20). This is a lifelong challenge that is modeled in the Old Testament example of Ezra.

Ezra ministered in a time of national renewal and restoration as the nation Israel returned from its exile in Babylon. Both Ezra, a representative of the clergy, and Nehemiah, a lay leader, were used by God to guide and to educate the people. In this work Ezra the priest and scribe devoted himself to the study of God's Word, to its observance, and to its teaching (Ezra 7:10). Christian believers make up a holy and royal priesthood who are to be dedicated in a similar way and thus offer spiritual sacrifices acceptable to God through Jesus Christ (1 Pet. 2:4–12). Dedication and commitment are required of those persons who constitute the priesthood of all believers today. Dedication is required in relation to the study of Scripture, to its being lived out, and to the ministry of teaching. This dedication provides an expression and a verification of believers' authority. The Scripture is central in the process of verification because it is the primary authority for understanding God's will for human and created life. The

Scripture is a witness to Christ, for in the written Word we encounter the living Word.

Application

Authority as derivative from God and Jesus Christ in the life of believers is related to God's revelation and human response to that revelation. Another Old Testament example is instructive of this relationship. Rahab, a harlot in Jericho, responded to the revelation she received from God. God had created a new people and established a new power, both of which confronted—or were revealed to—Rahab in the two spies who appeared on her doorstep. Rahab boldly cast off all allegiance to any other authority; she embraced the realm or rule of God and was a traitor to her city.[27] She received God's revelation and welcomed God's messengers in peace. Rahab made the right choice and was remembered for her action (Matt. 1:5; Heb. 11:31; James 2:25). Therefore she was recognized as one who could teach others by her faith. Rahab's faith was demonstrated through her works. The faith and works of believers provide a continuing foundation upon which teaching emerges. Without such works the reality of a living faith can be questioned. This is also the message of the New Testament Book of James, which teaches the essential relationship between faith and works that issue from that faith. Believers' works are visible expressions of a God who is still active in human and world history.

A continuing question for the faith community is the discernment of God's revelation. Rahab, in her trade as a prostitute, had others appear at her door. How did she discern the validity and reliability of the spies from Israel who implicitly claimed to represent God? How did she make the right choice of possible authoritative sources on the doorstep of her world? What can guide Christians today in discerning God's revelation with a host of available messages? Today we can affirm authoritative sources of the Scripture, church traditions and teachings, and experience. Our priority is given to Scripture. Human experience as Fackre describes it includes cognitive, affective, and moral or intentional

27. Andrew Johnson, "May 3, 1992," in *These Days* 32 (May-June 1992).

experience.[28] Discernment is not an easy task with a host of authorities seeking our allegiance today, but Jesus promised his presence and that of the Holy Spirit to guide us on our way in teaching and in all of life (Matt. 28:18–20; John 16:12–14). But even with the various sources for authority, the Christian must make choices as to their priority when confronting life situations.

The Reformation tradition has recognized the priority of Scripture, but not to the exclusion of tradition or human experience. The Reformation tradition of *semper reformanda* affirms the fact that Christians should always be open to the process of being reformed. Therefore Christians must be open to and discerning of new contours of God's work in the world. Such discernment poses challenges and problems not previously recognized along with an ever-present sense of adventure and wonder that can energize the fulfilling of God's mission by God's people. The fulfillment of that mission requires that Christians grapple with the place and use of authority in the church itself, the faith community (see chap. 2). The faith community is one context in which believers exercise their authority. God's fontal authority, the mediate authority of the Scripture, church tradition, and human experience—the community of faith wrestles with all these questions of theological authority in its effort to share authoritative teaching.

28. Fackre, *The Christian Story*, vol. 2, *Authority*, 133–56.

2

Authority in the Faith Community

The question of authority in the teaching ministry must be posed in the context of the faith community, the Christian church. This chapter explores the nature of institutional authority that builds upon the fontal authority residing in God and the mediate or theological authority residing primarily in the Scriptures, and secondarily in church traditions and human experience. In his recent work on authority Jackson W. Carroll observes:

> we cannot live together for long in any human community without submitting ourselves to the authority of the community's deepest values and norms and to the leadership of those charged with their articulation, interpretation, and realization. No community can function without some form of leadership that enables the community to survive and achieve its goals. Authority is no enemy of community, as we sometimes suppose. Rather, its enemies are tyranny, which coerces obedience without legitimacy; various forms of authoritarianism, which abuse authority;

and anarchy, in which each individual is an authority to him or herself.[1]

The exercise of authority assumes the presence of a group of persons who recognize the authority of a person, his or her office, or that person's function in a particular setting. Various communities in the Christian tradition place distinct emphasis on these three aspects of authority: persons, offices, and functions. In addition to these distinctions, models or paradigms of authority can be identified to describe and prescribe the exercise of authority in the church and the world. Christians must first consider authority within the faith community in relation to theology and, in particular, ecclesiology (the study of the church).

The Church in Which Authority Is Exercised

The Christian church was created by the Holy Spirit through the apostolic Word of Jesus Christ crucified; it was created at Pentecost by the redeeming Lord as the Spirit.[2] Those within the church must discern the working theology that serves to guide their mission. For example, Donald E. Messer has identified dysfunctional theologies that exist in the modern church. Dysfunctional theologies, Messer observes, "promote an individualistic ministry—one person responding to God's love with little regard for the community of faith."[3] Instead, Messer appropriately contends that Christian ministry is communitarian, the "expression of the gift of God as given via the church to the individual."[4] He also points out that power and authority are not directly bestowed on individuals, but on the congregation of Christians. Therefore the power and authority any person—clergy or laity—has is "gifted from God to the church to the person holding the

1. Jackson W. Carroll, *As One with Authority: Reflective Leadership in Ministry* (Louisville: Westminster/John Knox, 1991), 35.

2. P. T. Forsyth, *The Principle of Authority in Relation to Certainty, Sanctity and Society: An Essay in the Philosophy of Experiential Religion*, 2d ed. (London: Independent, 1952), 250.

3. Donald E. Messer, *A Conspiracy of Goodness: Contemporary Images of Christian Mission* (Nashville: Abingdon, 1992), 22.

4. Ibid.

given office."[5] Messer's emphasis on office must be complemented with consideration of both the person who occupies an
office and that person's function in the exercise of authority. But
Messer's emphasis on the communal character of authority must
be affirmed.

A functional theology of the church (ecclesiology) recognizes
the essential corporate dimension of the use or abuse of authority
by Christians. Without a sense of the "we" character of authority, the "me" preoccupation of the wider culture in the United
States creates a distortion of the gospel and biblical faith. Authority and power in Christian leadership are for the purpose of service within and beyond the Christian community and not for the
purpose of individual privilege and recognition. As the Scriptures
teach, the church is brought into being by the ministry of the
Holy Spirit (Acts 1; 1 Cor. 12) and with its multiple ministries it
functions as the body of Christ. All authority and power are given
to those gathered and scattered as the church for the common
good (1 Cor. 12:7) as persons serve God in relation to others and
their mission in the world.

In order to discern the proper use of their authority in the
church, Christians must clearly identify their mission. Their mission is given by God and their authority undergirds the fulfillment of that particular mission. Authority is a gift from God not
with the end of personal aggrandizement, but with the end of fulfilling God's mission in the world. The ultimate end of fulfilling
God's mission is glorifying and enjoying God forever. But the
question must then be asked in each setting: What is the church's
particular mission, of which teaching is one component? How is
teaching related to the broader mission of the church?

The Church's Mission

This question of mission is a difficult one. Mission can embrace all aspects of the life of the church. The word *mission* derives from the Latin *missio*, which means "to send." Authority is

5. Donald E. Messer, "Scattering the Gathered: Connecting Faith and Action," lecture presented at the National Association of Annual Conference of Lay
Leaders of the United Methodist Church, Nashville, Tennessee, 16–17 February,
1990, 2.

given to fulfill a mission upon which we are being sent, and that mission has particular purposes. We must ask ourselves where God is sending us and for what purpose or purposes. In the Gospel account of John 20:19–21, Jesus appears to his disciples after the resurrection and declares, "Peace be with you. As the Father has sent me, so I send you." As Jesus was sent by God on a unique mission, so disciples of Jesus are sent. This is an important beginning, but more must be said to define this mission. A number of authors make suggestions.

Paul D. Gehris and Katherine A. Gehris, in *The Teaching Church*, state that "mission is reaching out to others and into ourselves in whatever place or time, and with whatever resources we have available. . . . Mission is recognizing a need and responding out of our faith to the call to love one another."[6] This is a broad and inclusive definition, but subject to an important warning issued by Stephen Neill, a missiologist. In *Creative Tension*, Neill points out that "if everything is mission, nothing is mission."[7] If we define mission too broadly, we risk emptying this term of any substance and not providing clear guidance for the work of the church.

Arthur O. F. Bauer, a Lutheran mission educator, distinguishes between the task of the local church's ministry to its own membership (nurture, service, and fellowship within the Christian community itself) and mission to the community beyond.[8] In a similar way David R. Ray writes, "mission is all that the church does beyond its own maintenance and membership boundaries which seeds and nurtures faith, joy, peace, justice, health, love, freedom, self-sufficiency, and discipleship in the wider community here and throughout God's world.[9] Bauer and Ray see mission as comprehensive in the scope of activities, but both opt for a narrow locus that excludes the local congregation as a context for mission, although it is named as a context for ministry. Gab-

6. Paul D. Gehris and Katherine A. Gehris, *The Teaching Church—Active in Mission* (Valley Forge, Penn.: Judson, 1987), 54.

7. Stephen Neill, *Creative Tension* (London: Edinburgh House, 1959), 81.

8. Arthur O. F. Bauer, *Being in Mission: A Resource for the Local Church and Community* (New York: Friendship, 1987), 4–5.

9. David R. Ray, *Small Churches Are the Right Size* (New York: Pilgrim, 1982), 110.

riel Fackre also distinguishes the inreach and the outreach of the church. Preaching and teaching (*kerygma*), service or care within (*diakonia*), life together within (*koinonia*), and worship (*leitourgia*) all denote the inreach, nurture, or ministry of the church. The corresponding outreach tasks are evangelism (*kerygma*), social service and action without (*diakonia*), life together without (*koinonia*), and festival (*leitourgia*).[10] But it is also possible to conceive that Christians are called to a mission in their local church that is just as valid as work in the wider local, regional, national, or global community. In this case the local church itself becomes a context for mission or a mission outpost within the wider society. In this case the local church needs to receive missionaries who come from other contexts. A challenge presented to Christians in the light of this discussion is whether we should opt for a broad or a narrow definition of mission. A consideration of the history of thought about mission can help us in addressing this important question of the work of the church in the world.

In historical discussions of the church, Christians have stressed different facets of mission.[11] Some persons focused on proclamation or *kerygma*, the telling and retelling the Christian story, as central to mission. This group stressed the place of preaching, teaching, and evangelism. In relation to *kerygma*, teachers are to share the basic content of the gospel and to encourage a holistic response of persons to Jesus the Christ.

A second group focused on the formation of the community of faith and the place of fellowship or *koinonia*. In this second group the concern is for the experience of a welcoming, hospitable, caring, and healing community for both members and strangers. In relation to *koinonia*, teachers are to foster the formation of the faith community and the relational bonds among believers and God.

10. Gabriel Fackre, *The Christian Story: A Narrative Interpretation of Basic Christian Doctrine*, rev. ed. (Grand Rapids: Eerdmans, 1984), 171.

11. David J. Bosch explore these categories and a host of others in *Transforming Mission: Paradigm Shifts in Theology of Mission* (Maryknoll, N.Y.: Orbis, 1991), 368–510. Bosch's discussion is drawn upon in my exploration of the history.

A third has group emphasized the place of service (*diakonia*) and social outreach with the need to express faith in actions. For this third group the outworkings of the gospel in the local church, community, and society are indispensable. In relation to *diakonia*, those teaching are to encourage plans for and acts of service along with reflection upon what others have learned from their actions.

Combining these first three facets, a fourth group has equated mission with witness, *martyria*. A witness is given by the activities of proclamation, fellowship, and service. The term *witness* translates the Greek term *martys*, from which the term *martyr* also derives. In the New Testament the term is primarily applied to apostles who bear witness to the risen Christ (Acts 1:8). In the Book of Acts Jesus' parting words to his disciples before the ascension are reported: "But you will receive power when the Holy Spirit has come upon you; and you will be my witnesses in Jerusalem, in all Judea and Samaria, and to the ends of the earth." The apostles suffer gladly "for the name" (Acts 5:41; 9:16), yet it is by their life and missionary work that they bear witness to Christ. In their death they also witness, which is the connotation we usually give the word *martyr*.[12] In relation to *martyria*, teachers are to motivate and prepare active witnesses for Christ in the world.

A fifth group in ecumenical discussions has opted to stress the importance of worship and liturgy (*leitourgia*) as the central mission task of the church. For this group the distinctive of the church is the celebration of sacred time and space where God is glorified and honored. The central event of mission is the public worship service, and worship serves to distinguish the church from other social institutions. In relation to *leitourgia*, teachers are to foster a sense of reverence and awe in the lives of Christians and to consciously link educational efforts with the corporate and personal worship life of students.

A sixth and final group stressed the task of advocacy (*propheteia*), in which peace and justice are primary concerns in an unjust world at war. This group has sought to be an advocate for those who have been marginalized and oppressed and who need liberation. In relation to *propheteia*, teachers are to call forth and

12. P. H. Menoud, "Martyr," in *The Interpreter's Dictionary of the Bible*, ed. George A. Buttrick (Nashville: Abingdon, 1962), 288.

shape prophetic voices who advocate for God's values in the world and in church-related institutions.

Each of these six groups, along with others that combine these facets, can reduce the extent of the Christian mission to its preferred tasks. A challenge posed by the emphases of these various groups and voices is not to limit or to reduce God's mission. The perspective the author affirms is seeing mission as a multifaceted ministry that encompasses proclamation, fellowship, service, witness, worship, and advocacy. Mission includes the dimensions of inreach and outreach. What then prevents mission from being everything? The work of the late missiologist David Bosch provides insights in relation to this danger. Christians in each context must discern the contours of God's mission to which they are particularly called. This prevents mission from being everything and lacking focus.

Bosch, in *Transforming Mission*, argues that the process of defining mission is continual with the constant sifting, testing, and reformulating of its various facets. He therefore suggests the concept of "transforming mission." Transforming mission means both that mission is to be understood as an activity that transforms reality and that there is a constant need for mission itself to be transformed. Bosch cites the wisdom of James Russell Lowell, "New occasions teach new duties: time makes ancient good uncouth."[13]

One illustration of Bosch's insight is the changing description of the church's mission one finds in the Book of Acts. Life among believers included the tasks of proclamation, community formation or fellowship, and worship (Acts 2:42–47). But the needs of the church shifted to include more of an emphasis upon the need of *diakonia* or service (Acts 6:1–7). Service was not to the exclusion of other parts of the mission, but one aspect of mission has a specific point of urgency or emphasis at a particular time. A similar understanding is gained by appreciating a variety of views that the Gospels provide regarding the mission of Jesus.

The Gospels of Matthew, Mark, Luke, and John are four attempts at defining and redefining what the Christian church was

13. David J. Bosch, *Transforming Mission: Paradigm Shifts in Theology of Mission* (Maryknoll, N.Y.: Orbis, 1991), 47.

called to do and to be in faithfulness to the life and ministry of Jesus the Christ. In sharing the gospel message, each writer and each community in which the writer was living endeavored to define the mission of the church. Each Gospel presents a valid but distinct view of the gospel. Each group that is advocating a particular aspect of mission is to be affirmed. But each group must see and appreciate the expanse of mission and its changing contours along with its essential continuities. Such a perspective is necessitated by the fact that God is still active in the world and is calling the Christian church to follow after divine initiatives in each context. The emphasis of Christians upon being faithful to God in each particular context must be balanced with the emphasis upon fulfilling the universal purposes of God and the common mission of God in the world.

Bosch's insights in distinguishing mission and missions helps in maintaining that balance. Mission refers to *missio dei,* God's mission. In mission, God is revealed as the one who loves the world. Mission is God's involvement in and with the world. Mission is the nature and activity of God that embraces both the church and the world. Mission is God's mission in which the church is both called and privileged to participate. Mission celebrates the universal purposes of God for all of creation and humanity. A focus upon mission celebrates the unity and universality of God's work in the world. Missions, in contrast with mission, are *missiones ecclesiae,* the missionary ventures of the church in particular contexts. Missions refer to forms related to specific times, places, or needs. Missions are expressions of the church's participation in the *missio dei.* Missions celebrate the faithful response of the whole people of God in each community of believers.[14] We find in Bosch's work an attempt to balance the complementary themes of the particularity of missions and the universality of mission that is essential to maintain. Orlando E. Costas captured the universality of mission by observing that the church exists for mission, exists to tell, do, be, and celebrate the gospel (*kerygma, diakonia, koinonia, leitourgia*).[15]

14. Bosch, *Transforming Mission,* 10.
15. Orlando E. Costas, "The Mission and Nature of the Church," Andover Newton Theological School, Newton Centre, Massachusetts, 1986, 11.

Mission cannot be defined too narrowly or too sharply, nor too broadly. The definition of missions must be specific enough to clarify the faithful intentions and commitments of God's people in each setting. The definition of mission serves to clarify the universal purposes of God that must be reowned and reappropriated by each new generation. The definition of missions poses the challenge of incarnating the Christian faith in a particular time and place. In such incarnation the Christian church struggles with the dynamic between Christ and culture. The term *inculturation* has been suggested by Aylward Shorter of the Catholic Higher Institute of East Africa to note "the ongoing dialogue between faith and culture or cultures," or "the creative and dynamic relationship between the Christian message and a culture or cultures."[16] In its life and in its mission, each local church embodies an expression of faith in a particular culture or mix of cultures. For example, because of its different culture or subculture the church at Antioch (Acts 11:19–30; 13:1–3; 15:22–35) had a distinct, albeit complementary, mission as compared with that of the church in Jerusalem. The life within a local congregation represents the congregation's own subculture. Within that subculture the exercise of authority by both clergy and laity is related to the three aspects of persons, offices, and functions that serve to faithfully fulfill God's mission in the church and in the world. One essential aspect of God's mission is that of teaching (chap. 1). Teaching serves as a ministry of connection providing perspective on the relationships between the various tasks of proclamation, community formation, service, advocacy, and worship.[17]

Persons, Processes, and Positions

In 1981 Carroll reported on research that explored issues in clergy authority, but his work has implications for the ministry of laity as well. He defined authority as legitimate power. To exercise authority was to "control, direct, coordinate, or otherwise

16. Aylward Shorter, *Toward a Theology of Inculturation* (Maryknoll, N.Y.: Orbis, 1988), 11.

17. The nature of this connection is elaborated in Robert W. Pazmiño, *Principles and Practices of Christian Education: An Evangelical Perspective* (Grand Rapids: Baker, 1992), 37–57, 91–100.

guide the thought and behavior of persons and/or groups in ways that are considered legitimate by those persons and groups."[18] The research explored various dimensions of authority that help to discern the subculture of the local church in which authority is exercised.

Authority in ministry has its basis in one or two categories or in practice a combination of both categories. One category for the basis of authority emphasizes the person, clergy or lay leader, as a participant in the power of the *sacred*. The emphasis is on *whose we are* in the sense that the leader has a close relationship with God and therefore speaks for or represents God in the community. In relation to clergy this basis affirms the clergyperson as God's person or representative in the life of the faith community. Thus the leaders' authority is vitally connected with a holy or set-apart status. This set-apart status is for the purpose of service.

A second category emphasizes the person as possessor of professional or practical *expertise* necessary to the work of ministry. The emphasis is on *who we are* in the sense of possession of knowledge and skills needed to nurture the life of a religious group and its members. This category suggests that the person who serves as a leader has had the necessary training or education to qualify for service to a particular community.

In addition to the basis of authority, the degrees of institutionalization suggested two additional categories, one that emphasized the person and a second that emphasized the position. An emphasis on the person stresses that one particular individual possesses a set of gifts, characteristics, and/or abilities that qualify her or him to exercise authority. An emphasis on the position stresses that one occupies a particular office, an attribute of which is authority. But the authority of office and personal authority can be mutually reinforcing.[19]

A third category, not named by Carroll, can be suggested in terms of a process in which a person fulfills a unique function within a group or an institution. This function may not reside in any particular person or position, but nevertheless is essential to

18. Jackson W. Carroll, "Some Issues in Clergy Authority," *Review of Religious Research* 23 (December 1981): 99–108. Carroll's work is drawn upon in what follows. His earlier work is expanded upon in *As One with Authority*.
19. Carroll, *As One with Authority*, 57.

the life of the community. In this case distinctions of authority and leadership are more functional than substantive. Process stresses the relational dimensions of authority where one positively influences others in achieving group goals and developing the commitment of others.

In plotting out the two bases of authority and the three degrees of institutionalization, one can propose six distinct types of authority that function in different communities (see table 1). Each type represents one possible combination of the two dimensions of authority, namely, bases of authority and degrees of institutionalization. One must recognize that any particular setting may represent a combination of these ideal types and that leaders may operate at several levels simultaneously. But each community tends to embody one dominant understanding of authority as suggested by each of the ideal types.

Table 1
Types of Authority

		Sacred *Whose We Are*	Expertise *Who We Are*
Degrees of Institutionalization	Person	1 Parson	4 Professional
	Process	2 Watchperson	5 Facilitator
	Position	3 Priest/ess	6 Elder

Bases of Authority

Type 1 emphasizes the sacred base of authority that resides in a person. In this community configuration a person with authority has demonstrated the power of the Holy Spirit in his or her life and ministry. This person has a special relationship with God. The leader in this case is the parson, understood historically as "God's person" who uniquely represents God for the community. This authority has been common in the Pentecostal, Quaker, Anabaptist, and free-church traditions along with charismatic movements that have valued charisma evidenced in the lives and ministries of leaders.

Type 2 emphasizes the function of individuals who foster God's mission in the church and the world. They foster a process of taking stock and launching out, often in a visionary way. These persons are the watchmen and the watchwomen, those who rally others to be, to become, and to minister at God's bidding. Type 2 authority has been common in both parachurch and various missional structures. The emphasis is not so much on the charisma that a person possesses over time, but on how God uses the person to address a particular need in the life of the community. That need may be associated with a time of transition or crisis when the watchperson serves the community.

Type 3 emphasizes the sacred base that resides in the office or position one occupies in the church. This type of authority emphasizes the leader as a priest or a priestess. By assuming a sacred position named and recognized by the religious community one is granted the privilege and the responsibility of exercising authority. This sacramental power is usually conferred in ordination upon one who occupies a pastoral or governing office. This authority has been common in the Roman Catholic, Episcopal, and Orthodox traditions and in other churches that embrace episcopal polity.

Type 4 emphasizes the base of expertise or knowledge that an individual possesses. Authority is granted and recognized in those who are professionals and who have been certified on the basis of advanced study, training, or experience. This authority has been common for those who serve as denominational executives or professors in theological schools and seminaries. Usually a professional guild serves to recognize those who qualify as authorities and to foster the recognition of expertise.

Type 5 stresses the base of expertise in relation to fostering an ongoing process in the life of an institution, a group, or a community. Persons who function with this authority have been trained as facilitators, consultants, change agents, and community organizers who initiate, develop, and bring to fruition a process necessary for the ongoing life of a community. This authority has been common in the formation and reformation of various institutions and communities. When old patterns or forms are no longer functional, groups look for persons who can assist in the process of discerning and implementing new possibilities. Their credentials and track record serve to certify their expertise.

Type 6 emphasizes expertise that resides in an institutional officeholder and is therefore conferred on the person who occupies that office by virtue of the process that places him or her in that position. This authority is given to those who serve in a representative fashion for the entire community or institution. This authority is common in the Presbyterian tradition in which the pastor serves as the teaching elder and is distinct from the ruling elders. All those named and recognized as elders represent this ideal type. Teaching elders have acquired the required expertise to occupy their office and those occupying the office are respected and authorized to decide and act.

One additional factor named by Carroll in his research on clergy authority is crucial: the relational dimension. This dimension explores the symmetry or asymmetry that exists in clergy-laity relations. A similar comparison can be suggested in relation to teachers and students. Three potential expressions of symmetry or asymmetry can be observed. First, symmetrical authority relationships exist where power within the religious or educational system is, in principle, available to all members, thus fostering mutuality. In the extreme case of symmetrical relationships, no one member has authority over others (see the discussion on autonomy). All share equally in power and have the right to exercise it; the distinctions between clergy and laity or teachers and students are eliminated. Second, where relatively symmetrical relationships exist, distinctions between clergy and laity are functional rather than substantive and absolute; that is, clergy or teachers are granted authority in some areas within or on behalf of the system on the agreement that it is for the good of the whole. Third, an asymmetrical authority relationship occurs where clergy and teachers are viewed as having access to power that is restricted and generally unavailable to laity or students respectively. Asymmetrical authority relationships are typically outgrowths of periods in which social relationships are hierarchically ordered, whereas symmetrical relationships tend to develop as egalitarian values come to the fore, often in reaction against hierarchy. Carroll suggests that the Christian gospel "moves us in the direction of symmetry and a complementarity of gifts within the ministry of the whole people of God."[20] The Christian gospel moves us in the direction of one of three models of authority.

The six types of authority serve to distinguish how authority is generally perceived in various communities, a perception that may or may not equate with how authority actually functions. The six types help to distinguish dominant and secondary community expectations for those who exercise authority. But pastoral leaders are generally expected to give evidence of spirituality (a relationship with God) and expertise along with functional verification of their calling. In other words, while being a representative of the sacred and having a distinctive expertise that is certified in ordination (authority of office), clergy must demonstrate in practice their calling (personal authority).[21] A concern for practice suggests the need to consider the actual functioning of authority in faith communities. The work of Letty M. Russell is helpful in exploring functional models of authority that operate in all forms of ministry.

Three Models of Authority

Russell suggests that three models for authority have been operative in the life of the Christian church. The three models she names are those of *paternalism* (I would add maternalism), *autonomy*, and *partnership*.[22] These three models can be further elaborated upon in relation to both personal and public expressions of authority. Paternalism/maternalism can be identified as heteronomy, which is the state of being subject to an authority of the other that may include father, mother, or one's family, church, community, or nation.

Heteronomy

Paternalism or maternalism represents the exercise of authority over others and over the community with the dominant interest of control. This stance has also been named hegemony; it

20. Ibid., 78.
21. Ibid., 54, 120–21.
22. While naming maternalism, I recognize the presence of patriarchy in both the Christian church and most societies. But this is not exclusively the case.

embodies asymmetrical and hierarchical relationships. In the case of children and others who lack adequate personal control, the exercise of this authority can serve to protect individual persons and others from serious injury and loss. But the exclusive use of this authority can result in a false love that encourages dependence, inferiority, and domination.[23]

Paternal and maternal care are to be affirmed for the adequate growth and early development of persons, but parents expect that children will internalize controls and eventually function in ways that do not endanger themselves or others. Two dangers exist in heteronomy: tyranny and authoritarianism. In tyranny those with illegitimate authority coerce the obedience of others. In authoritarianism those with legitimate authority abuse it.[24]

The inappropriate exercise of paternalism or maternalism in teaching results in what the Brazilian educator Paulo Freire called banking education. Freire observes that the main transaction in banking education is transference of information from the teacher's head to the heads of the students. This process, in which the teacher assumes an authoritarian role, can be described as prescriptive and directive. Freire identifies ten characteristics of banking education:

1. The teacher teaches, the students are taught.
2. The teacher knows all, the students know nothing.
3. The teachers think, the students are thought about.
4. The teacher talks, the students listen meekly.
5. The teacher disciplines, the students are disciplined.
6. The teacher chooses, the students comply.
7. The teacher acts, the students have the illusion of acting.
8. The teacher selects the content, the students adapt to it.
9. The teacher imposes professional authority, the students lose their freedom.
10. The teacher is the subject, the students are mere objects.[25]

23. Letty M. Russell, "Authority in Mutual Ministry," *Quarterly Review* 6 (Spring 1986): 14–16.
24. Carroll, *As One with Authority*, 35.
25. Paulo Freire, *Pedagogy of the Oppressed*, trans. Myra Bergman Ramos (New York: Seabury, 1970), 59.

The result of such teaching, as Freire suggests, is oppression. The teacher's control results in a relationship of dependence that is maintained regardless of the abilities or the maturity of the students. Banking education does not foster dialogue and the full participation of students as active persons.

One danger of characterizing teaching in such a way is to discount the teacher's essential sharing of wisdom with students, a process that can occur without imposition. This appropriate sharing allows students the freedom to disagree and to jointly search for truth. The stance of paternalism/maternalism or heteronomy maintains the predominant influence and authority of an external presence over others. This sense of being over others assumes the existence of a hierarchy or at least a dominant-subordinate relationship. Jesus warns about this model of leadership in Luke 22: 25–27:

> The kings of the Gentiles lord it over them; and those in authority over them are called benefactors. But not so with you; rather the greatest among you must become like the youngest, and the leader like the one who serves. For who is greater, the one who is at table or the one who serves? Is it not the one at the table? But I am among you as one who serves.

Autonomy

The second model of authority Russell identifies is that of autonomy: persons maintain a stance of authority within themselves. A radical stance of authority results in a perceived freedom to be oneself in radical symmetrical and egalitarian relationships. This freedom can result in the lack of an experience of interpersonal love and community. Moreover, this radical stance prohibits persons from moving beyond themselves and connecting with significant others. The values of independence, self-sufficiency, and invulnerability dissolve into personal, communal, and social isolation.[26] The danger Carroll named in relation to autonomy is anarchy, wherein each individual is an authority to himself or herself.[27] Strivings for independence and

26. Russell, "Authority in Mutual Ministry," 16–17.
27. Carroll, *As One with Authority*, 35.

individual identity are to be affirmed in both human and educational development, but autonomy can lead to a destructive individualism that rips the fabric of human life, which is inherently communal and social.

One expression of this dangerous trend toward individualism is the exclusive emphasis on self-directed and individualized learning. This form of learning has been facilitated by technological advancements that allow for programmed and computer-assisted modules. Another development has been the rise of andragogy, the art and science of helping adults learn, and contracted learning, which for some persons has provided access not previously afforded to educational resources. The potential weakness of exclusive reliance upon such forms is that they may not foster the connections essential for human community and social responsibility. Some persons prefer to learn in limited association with other persons, whereas some persons need regular interaction and dialogue with peers and those who serve as instructors or mentors. We can recognize these preferences, but the challenge posed for any educational program is to foster a sense of mutual relationship and accountability with other persons and various publics. Thus the challenge is to move persons beyond a stance of autonomy to one of interdependence. The biblical example of John Mark's independent desertion of Paul and Barnabas (Acts 13:13) and Paul's eventual petition for his services (2 Tim. 4:11) as an interdependent partner in the ministry suggests that such a move is possible.[28] The dangers of individualism must be countered with a concern for the wider human and ecological community. Dangers also exist in an exclusive emphasis on communitarianism that does not allow for the emergence of individuals. But the greater danger exists in the United States of a destructive personalism and an individualism that has diminished a sense of the commonweal. P. T. Forsyth observed that

> In Christian religion independence is not the way to authority, but authority to independence. We do not first become our own moral masters and then accept the Savior. We do not cultivate

28. Ronald Habermas and Klaus Issler, *Teaching for Reconciliation: Foundations and Practice of Christian Education Ministry* (Grand Rapids: Baker, 1992), 268.

the spiritual virtues and then mark and admire their consummation in Christ. . . . It is Christ's authority as Savior that gives us to ourselves, and His service makes us our own free [persons]. Christian obedience means actual obedience to an authority we have found, and found only because it first finds us; it is not merely a willingness to obey if our authority could be found. To obey Christ thus is better than to be free; it is the only way to be permanently free, individually or socially; and without such obedience freedom is a curse. *Absolute* obedience [to God] is the condition of *entire* freedom.[29]

The emphasis upon autonomy and independence is a welcome alternative to heteronomy, but it fails to recognize the social and corporate nature of created life that is named in the Christian model of partnership.

Partnership

The third model of authority described by Russell is that of partnership. She defines partnership as an "authority of freedom that uses people's need for solidarity and care to empower them through a relationship of mutuality."[30] Russell sees authority as the freedom to participate with others in a community of mutual caring, companionship, and interdependence. Authority can be understood as authorizing the inclusion of all persons as partners, and power is understood as empowerment for self-actualization with others.[31] The emphasis upon self-actualization is necessary to avoid the dangers of the loss of individuality in a stance of hegemony. The emphasis upon self-actualization with others is necessary in order to avoid the dangers of the loss of community in a stance of autonomy. The commitment to and experience of interdependence foster the growth of community, foster life within a household of freedom. According to Russell, such households exist where mutual love, care, and trust are present.[32] Russell advocates the partnership model and suggests it is demonstrated for

29. Forsyth, *Principle of Authority*, 272.
30. Ibid., 17.
31. Letty M. Russell, *Household of Freedom: Authority in Feminist Theology* (Philadelphia: Westminster, 1987), 37, 61.
32. Ibid., 87.

us in the community life of Jesus and his disciples. Both symmetrical and asymmetrical relationships can be cited in the relationship of Jesus with his disciples. But the partnership model is best represented for us in life of the Trinity as Creator, Redeemer, and Sustainer.

Carroll discusses partnership in terms of reflective leadership: "The authority of the reflective leader resides in her or his ability to assist partners in ministry to form a vision of Christian existence and construct responses that are both faithful to that vision and appropriate within the complex, messy situations of practice."[33]

The partnership Russell and Carroll discuss can be realized only in a stance of theonomy in which we are subject and obedient to God's authority. But it is essential to note that theonomy that is distinct from autonomy is also distinct from heteronomy. As Forsyth observed:

> The God who rules us in Christ is not a foreign power. Theonomy is not heteronomy. He, our law, becomes also our life. He comes with something more even than authority over us, he comes with power in us. His authority is not simply impressive, it is enabling. . . . It is the power of the Spirit, not revealing alone, but redeeming us to take in the revelation. His Spirit does not seize us but lives in us. The Savior Son is revealed in us. Christ is our life who is also our Lord. His authority is not simply an external power, but a life-giving spirit within. We are redeemed into the power to know, to be, and to do what is revealed.[34]

Theonomy enables us to move from the stances of dependence and independence to interdependence with God and others. Being subject and obedient to God in theonomy leads to true freedom that is sought in autonomy and the grounding and structure sought in heteronomy. Being subject and obedient to God in theonomy empowers one for partnership.

This third model of authority that stresses mutuality implies for teaching and learning a mediating position in relation to two dominant educational approaches. The traditional teacher-

33. Carroll, *As One with Authority*, 153–54.
34. P. T. Forsyth, *The Gospel and Authority: A P. T. Forsyth Reader*, ed. Marvin W. Anderson (Minneapolis: Augsburg, 1971), 23.

directed approach described by Freire as banking education provides access to content and continuity with the expectations of the community or society, but may squelch students and limit their discovery of the truth. The teacher-directed approach stresses a received perspective in which the knowledge and traditions from the past are honored. In this perspective the received culture is affirmed or taken rather than critiqued or made. As a result students are maintained in a stance of dependence.

The newer student-directed approach focuses on student interests and needs, but may ignore the insights provided by being attentive to traditional content and the norms of the community or society. As compared with a teacher-directed approach, the student-directed approach stresses a reflexive perspective in which the needs and interests of the students are given priority. In this perspective the received culture is critiqued with the hope of establishing or making a new culture that is relevant to the world of the students.[35] A student-directed approach stresses the independence of students; as a result students are isolated from the past and the community.

Authority in teaching is best modeled where mutuality can be established between teachers and students, between a teacher-directed approach and a student-directed approach. This mediating position also has implications for how curriculum is conceived and practiced.[36] A mutually-directed approach works toward a stance of interdependence for both teachers and students, a stance that recognizes the contributions of the past and the possibilities for the present and the future.

In *A Teachable Spirit*, Richard R. Osmer identifies a number of authorities that operate in relation to the teaching office in the church and its recovery. They include ministers, church councils, congregations, theologians, individual conscience, and church tradition. These various authorities are to work in partnership to discern the truth that is to be taught. But Osmer argues that their teaching authority is dependent on their faithfulness to Scripture

---

35. For a discussion of these in relationship to theology see Robert W. Pazmiño, *Foundational Issues in Christian Education: An Introduction in Evangelical Perspective* (Grand Rapids: Baker, 1988), 63–68.

36. Ibid., 210–14.

because "no single church authority can be raised to a position that rivals that of the Bible."[37]

The advocacy of partnership must affirm the primacy of Scripture to guide the church's faith and life. The church stands in a unique relationship to the Bible. As Lesslie Newbigin notes,

> The Bible functions as authority only within a community that is committed to faith and obedience and is embodying that commitment in an active discipleship that embraces the whole of life, public and private. . . . It is not the Bible itself but the church confessing the mystery of faith that is spoken of as the pillar and bulwark of the truth (1 Timothy 3:15–16).[38]

Therefore, for the church to teach with authority a working partnership is needed that includes ministers, church councils, theologians, believers with their individual consciences, and the voices of church tradition as each of these agents interprets the Scriptures. The mutuality practiced in this partnership assures the continued faithfulness and authority of Christian teaching. Osmer notes that the Holy Spirit is the primary teacher of the church with the written Word as the Spirit's basic subject matter. The Spirit is bound to the Word and attests to its authority. The Word serves to help believers test the insights attributed to the Spirit.[39] With this partnership in mind, Osmer names the three central teaching tasks of the church that serve to clarify the particular mission to which teachers are called in partnership with God and others:

> (1) the determination of the normative beliefs and practices of the church, (2) the reinterpretation of these beliefs and practices in shifting cultural and historical contexts, and (3) the formation and sustenance of educational institutions, processes, and curricula by which the church's normative beliefs and practices are taught, allowing them to be appropriated meaningfully by

37. Richard R. Osmer, *A Teachable Spirit: Recovering the Teaching Office in the Church* (Louisville: Westminster/John Knox, 1990), 119.

38. Lesslie Newbigin, *Foolishness to the Greeks: The Gospel and Western Culture* (Geneva: World Council of Churches; Grand Rapids: Eerdmans, 1986), 58.

39. Osmer, *A Teachable Spirit*, 110.

each new generation and grasped with deeper understanding by individuals.[40]

Within the framework of these larger central tasks, or in other words the educational mission, the authority of the Christian teacher in the local setting can be understood.[41] Donald G. Emler suggests that there are two levels of authority in the teaching act. First, there is the authority of the larger community as it determines the metacurriculum that Osmer names, the central and perennial teaching tasks of the Christian church. Second, there is the authority of the classroom teacher as she or he implements the teaching. The Christian teacher represents the faith community in the teaching act. The Christian teacher incarnates the community's story in the teaching setting as well as in the life of the community, seeking to enable persons to own and live out the Christian faith.[42]

Thus the Christian teacher is in partnership with the larger local and global faith community that down through the ages and into the future teaches the faith. In that task the teacher's authority is undergirded by the authority of the triune God who is in partnership with redeemed humankind, some of whom are gifted for teaching. As Paul observed in his epistle to the Ephesians (4:7–8):

> But each of us was given grace according to the measure of Christ's gift. Therefore it is said,

> "When he ascended on high he made captivity itself a captive;
> he gave gifts to his people."

One of those gifts is that of teaching. Chapter 3 will explore the authority of one's person and gifts in teaching.

---

40. Ibid., 15.
41. For a detailed discussion of the educational tasks of the church see Robert W. Pazmiño, *Principles and Practices of Christian Education: An Evangelical Perspective* (Grand Rapids: Baker, 1992), 45–57, 91–115.
42. Donald G. Emler, *Revisioning the DRE* (Birmingham, Ala.: Religious Education Press, 1989), 167.

3

Authority of One's Person and Gifts

Teaching in the Christian community is a gift of the Holy Spirit. In order to understand the authority of their persons and gifts in teaching, Christian teachers must consider dimensions of their spirituality. Spirituality in Christian faith centers upon one's relationship with the Holy Spirit, the third person of the Trinity. In discussing spirituality, Christians must be warned by P. T. Forsyth: "to put spirituality in the place of justification is to vaporise the Church."[1] Spirituality must be understood in relation to the justification offered by the grace of God in the death and resurrection of Jesus Christ. Theological grounding is crucial in exploring spirituality and fostering teaching that is spiritually anointed.

1. P. T. Forsyth, *The Principle of Authority in Relation to Certainty, Sanctity and Society: An Essay in the Philosophy of Experiential Religion*, 2d ed. (London: Independent, 1952), 348.

Contemporary interest in spirituality is rampant, and Christians must be discerning in both their thought and practice about a spirituality appropriate to the foundations of their faith, a spirituality appropriate for authoritative teaching. Justo L. Gonzalez, a church historian, has aptly observed that spirituality "has to do with the manner in which the gospel is both 'lived in' and 'lived out.' Spirituality is first of all living in the gospel—making faith the foundation for life. And it is also living out the gospel—making faith the foundation of action and structure."[2] If teachers hope to discern and nurture their spiritual life and that of their students, they must explore how the gospel of Jesus Christ is to be both personally and corporately lived in and lived out. They must also be clear in establishing the foundations for Christian life and teaching (chaps. 1–2).[3] Teachers must be discerning of their existing spirituality and the spirituality that pervades the entire faith community in which they are serving. This discernment and the actual enjoyment of a dynamic spiritual life in communion with God protect the well drawn upon in Christian teaching.

Existing Spiritualities

An ecumenical study of spiritual formation conducted by the Programme on Theological Education of the World Council of Churches in 1987 observed that all persons, all teachers, and all church leaders have some sort of spirituality.

It may be bland, selfish, destructive or downright demonic, but every one of us has what Augustine would call an *ordo amoris* (order of loves). Our spirituality is not what we explicitly express, nor what we profess to believe, but how we order our loves. That ordering may be unarticulated, even quite unconscious, but the resultant spirituality pervades our whole life and involves our whole person. Our stewardship of time, energy, and

2. Justo L. González, *Mañana: Christian Theology from a Hispanic Perspective* (Nashville: Abingdon, 1990), 157.
3. For further discussion of foundational issues in relation to Christian teaching, see Robert W. Pazmiño, *Foundational Issues in Christian Education: An Introduction in Evangelical Perspective* (Grand Rapids: Baker, 1988).

substance reflects the way we live out and express the ordering of our loves. . . . There can be and indeed is what can be called a spirituality of consumerism, a spirituality of security, a spirituality of the avoidance of pain, or even a spirituality of destructive violence.[4]

A diversity of spiritualities exists and the important prior step in nurturing spirituality is to be discerning of the existing spiritualities that pervade our lives, the lives of those who are leaders, and the life of the faith community in which we serve.

By discerning existing spiritualities of persons in a local church or ministry, Christian teachers are better able to affirm and/or confront those loves that order the inner and outer faith life of themselves and of students alike. A concern for the order of our loves and lives implies an interest in discipleship, discipline, and stewardship to which all Christians are called. For Christians the order of our loves is indicated in the biblical great commandment: to love the Lord our God with all of our heart, soul, mind, and strength and to love our neighbor as ourselves (Mark 12:30–31). While confronting the diverse false spiritualities and loves of our age, Christian teachers must recognize and celebrate the genuine expressions of Christian spirituality that are present in their lives and those of others. This is also a challenge for those who serve as leaders and who undergird the ministries of teachers. Although they live in an age of criticism and cynicism, spiritual leaders must consciously and consistently nurture a stance of affirmation among teachers. Constant criticism of others can limit them to their past, whereas appropriate affirmation can release them to the possibilities of present and future ministry.[5]

In relation to the teaching ministry, it is essential for leaders to identify and share the particulars of Christian spirituality. It is also essential for teachers to understand and to incarnate

---

4. *Spiritual Formation in Theological Education: An Invitation to Participate* (Geneva: Programme on Theological Education, World Council of Churches, 1987), 8.

5. This insight was shared by Rev. James Cyr of Scotch Plains, New Jersey, in relation to the impact of criticism and prayer as derived from the work of Marshall Shelley, *Well-Intentioned Dragons: Ministering to Problem People in the Church* (Carol Stream, Ill.: Christianity Today; Waco: Word, 1985), 123.

these particulars first in their lives and then in their ministries. In this way they will be able to teach with the authority bestowed by God's Spirit. Authority in spiritual teaching is conditioned by what we are and become in our spiritual lives, but is also unconditionally dependent upon God's power at work within us through the promptings and indwelling of the Holy Spirit.

Christian Spirituality

In the Bible we recognize a great diversity of spiritual life that directly relates to the particular context and experience of God's people. Different traditions of faith and experience fostered different spiritualities. This can be seen particularly in the Old Testament with its broad historical perspective.[6] The peculiar spirituality of the pilgrim people of the exodus tradition emphasized faithfulness to God's covenant in the midst of change and conflict. God called a people to lifelong commitment in the formation of a new community; in response, Joshua and his household committed themselves to serve the Lord (Josh. 24:15). The royal traditions of the united, then divided, kingdoms of Israel and Judah required faithfulness to God's values of righteousness and justice in the political, economic, and social affairs of state (Ps. 72; Isa. 58).

The priestly traditions in Jerusalem emphasized a spirituality that was sustained even after the exile and that was modeled in the lives of both Nehemiah the lay leader and Ezra the priest. Ezra was dedicated to the study, living out, and teaching of God's Word (Ezra 7:10); the same dedication should characterize those called to teaching today. The wisdom spirituality of the sages required a wholehearted listening and whole-life response to wisdom as she called to persons in their daily walk (Prov. 8). Those who waited upon wisdom discovered fullness and joy in life despite their struggles and trials. This is particularly the case with the *anawim*, whose spirituality challenges a culture of materialism and individualism.

---

6. *Spiritual Formation in Christian Education*, 9. My discussion elaborates upon the Old Testament examples cited in the World Council study.

62

The Anawim

The spirituality of the *anawim* (those who are poor, humble, and weak before God and others) was distinctive and is of particular significance for the majority of Christians across the globe. Even though the *anawim* represented the marginal groups of society, they were frequently used by God to exhibit valued models of spiritual life instructive to the whole people of God and therefore their deeds are recorded in Scripture. What lessons can Christians today learn from this providential plan in biblical history?

The spirituality of the *anawim* is incarnated in their lives and actions. A number of examples can be cited. Hagar, the pregnant Egyptian maidservant of Sarah and Abraham, demonstrated a radical trust in God for the life of Ishmael, even though she had been mistreated and sent away. Rahab, a harlot in Jericho, offered sanctuary to the Hebrew spies, chose loyalty to God above allegiance to her city-state, and thus saved her household. She is listed among Jesus' ancestors (Matt. 1:5). Ruth is also named in Matthew's genealogy of Jesus; she was a foreign widow who remained faithful to her mother-in-law, Naomi. Ruth trusted in God's provision even when she was gleaning to survive. The Hebrew midwives in Egypt (Exod. 1:15–22) saved the lives of male children and subverted Pharaoh's plans of destruction. They jeopardized their own lives to save the lives of newborn children. The widow at Zarephath (1 Kings 17) risked all and offered her last meal to Elijah when she and her son were at the point of death. Naaman's wife had a Hebrew girl servant. This servant suggested who might offer healing to her master, a healing that was realized when Naaman sought out Elisha (2 Kings 5). The lepers who camped outside the city gate of Samaria risked surrender to the enemy and discovered that the Aramean army was routed (2 Kings 7). They realized the selfishness of their initial response in enjoying the spoils left by the army and shared the good news of their discovery with those remaining in the besieged city.

Such were the *anawim*, those who were marginal in society but open to new possibilities of spiritual renewal. Through their sacrificial acts they demonstrated their spirituality and their higher accountability to God. Along with the host of witnesses in Hebrews 11, they serve as models who taught by their way of faith, life, and love. The New Testament books that best describe Jesus' continued ministry with the *anawim* are Luke, Acts, and Philemon. In Jesus' earthly ministry and in the New Testament church, those marginal to society are called to be disciples and to express their spirituality in diverse ways. For example, when Jesus was ridiculed for the company he kept—tax collectors, harlots, publicans, and sinners—he never challenged those statements. In his earthly ministry he preferred to be with these people rather than the recognizably religious. Jesus' intentional plan was to be with those who acknowledged their need of a physician (i.e., the *anawim*).

Attending to the example of the *anawim*, Christian teachers must discern what in a given time and place is the faithful way of worshiping, witnessing to, and serving God. All true Christian spiritualities help those who follow Christ to walk and live in God's presence with body, mind, and soul. They help to maintain hope in the midst of the sufferings and struggles of this world.[7] This is particularly evidenced in the lives of the *anawim*, but in others as well throughout the Scriptures. Hebrews 11 recounts the persons of faith who risked all to encounter and follow God despite the extremity of their circumstances (as judged by human standards). The stance of vulnerability and the willingness to seek an alternative graciously offered by God made the difference. The stance of utter dependence upon God for one's very life and daily survival can lead to a dynamic spiritual life that readily communicates to others one's willingness to follow Christ.

"Christian spirituality encompasses all authentic ways of *following Christ*. It is a pilgrimage to God through Christ, a process of sanctification, a process of being formed in the image of God through Jesus Christ."[8] The call to Christian teachers, like the call to all believers, is to live by faith as did the *anawim*. The righteous will live by faith. In the gospel a righteousness from God is revealed, a righteousness that is by faith and that is made available in Jesus Christ (Rom. 1:16–17). Christian spirituality for teachers implies a discipleship centered upon Jesus Christ as Lord and a walk with Christ's Spirit, the Holy Spirit. This discipleship

7. Ibid., 9–10.
8. Ibid., 10.

with Christ and the daily walk with the Holy Spirit provide the basis for authority in one's person and gifts in teaching.

Discipleship with Jesus Christ

Discipleship is essential to Christian spirituality and teaching. But, in contrast with generic spirituality, discipleship is never self-centered or self-occupied. Christian discipleship is always other-centered; oriented to the way of Jesus and the community of his followers.[9] The gift of teaching is a spiritual gift given for the common good (1 Cor. 12:7). The loss of perspective toward the common good must be addressed by all those who teach in the Christian church, clergy and laity. Clarity with regard to the what and why of Christian teaching must be a priority among those who serve in teaching ministries. This clarity is assured through exploring the foundational issues in Christian education, a task required of each generation of Christians.[10] Beyond the common good that each local church must identify, appropriate, and live out, educational leaders and teachers can explore the particulars of discipleship.

Marianne Sawicki, in *The Gospel in History*, identifies four particulars of discipleship that relate to teaching. They are a personal encounter with Jesus; a call to which one responds; a mission to testify to others about Jesus; and a following of Jesus to death.[11] Each of these has implications for nurturing the spiritual life of teachers.

First and foremost, *Christian teachers must have a personal faith encounter with Jesus and a commitment to follow Jesus Christ as Lord of their lives and teaching ministries.* This is basic, but requires the careful attention of those who recruit persons to serve as teachers. Beyond this initial commitment, teachers are re-

9. Ibid.
10. See Pazmiño, *Foundational Issues in Christian Education*, for an exploration of foundational issues. Also see Ronald Habermas and Klaus Issler, *Teaching for Reconciliation: Foundations and Practice of Christian Educational Ministry*, part 1, "Educational Ministry Foundations" (Grand Rapids: Baker, 1992).
11. Marianne Sawicki, *The Gospel in History: Portrait of a Teaching Church: The Origins of Christian Education* (New York: Paulist, 1988), 60, 62, 90.

quired to deepen and strengthen their relationship with Jesus. Leaders must attend to the nurture of the nurturers in the church. Teachers who do not regularly attend corporate worship are at particular risk, as are those who do not regularly nourish their own souls through personal Bible study, prayer, and devotion.

Second, *Christian teachers need to discern the particular nature of their call to teach and to develop their gifts of teaching as a part of that unique spiritual call.* James W. Fowler helpfully elaborates upon the consequences of understanding our lives in terms of our Christian call or vocation. The consequences include the following:

- People realize that their vocational callings are unique. Competition with others is reduced.
- We are freed from the anxiety that someone else might fulfill our particular calling.
- We rejoice in God's grace and favor in others, and we are not threatened by them.
- We are freed from the false guilt to be "all things to all people." We find comfort in God's plan that we each have a task to perform. Nothing more; nothing less; nothing to sidetrack us.
- We are released from self-vindicating thoughts and behavior. We don't need to prove our worth. We seek the balance of time and energy in all of life's responsibilities (family, culture, and church).
- The tyranny of time itself no longer incarcerates us. We are given God's grace in life—even in death.[12]

A call to teach children, for example, requires sensitivities and abilities distinct from those required to teach youth or adults. The call to teach may also involve openness to work cooperatively on a teaching team that requires complementing the gifts of other teachers. The call to teach implies an openness to the evaluation

12. See Ronald Habermas and Klaus Issler, *Teaching for Reconciliation: Foundations and Practice of Christian Educational Ministry* (Grand Rapids: Baker, 1992), 183, as derived from James W. Fowler, *Becoming Adult, Becoming Christian: Adult Development and Christian Faith* (San Francisco: Harper and Row, 1984), 103–5.

of the content, process, and results of teaching in relation to the common good of the local ministry.[13] In all of these areas educational and pastoral leaders nurture the spiritual lives of teachers by providing opportunities for self- and group evaluations. Leaders also organize occasions for the appropriate celebration of what has been accomplished by the grace of God. Teachers need support and recognition for their efforts and encouragement for the continued outworking of their call.

Third, *teachers need opportunities to be equipped or trained in fulfilling their mission to teach.* Various teaching skills can be improved through practice, and teachers can develop more creative and innovative styles if freedom is provided to test new ideas and to explore options. Teachers need occasions to be in fellowship with other teachers and to realize that others encounter the problems they experience. Teachers may also need to explore how their teaching can enable students to hear the gospel afresh and to respond faithfully to the claims of Jesus Christ upon their lives. Various teacher-training events must also include times to fellowship with the master teacher Jesus and to gain perspective in terms of the values and virtues of Christ's reign.

Fourth, *discipleship in Christian teaching implies a willingness to follow Jesus to death.* Dietrich Bonhoeffer noted that when Christ calls a person, he bids one to come and die.[14] Some teachers view their ministry as a call to martyrdom because of their challenging classroom experiences! But the word *martyr* actually derives from the verb *to witness.* Christian teachers are called to witness to the life-transforming power of the risen Lord not only with their teachings about Jesus, but also with their lives. To "follow Jesus to death" requires that teachers be challenged with the lifelong denial of self, so that the life of Christ is manifested within the classrooms and other settings for Christian teaching. Educational and pastoral leaders are to issue and model that challenge. Such a challenge can be fulfilled only by walking in and with the Holy Spirit.

13. I identify the specific areas for such an evaluation of teachin in *Principles and Practices of Christian Education: An Evangelical Perspective,* chap. 6, "Educational Evaluation" (Grand Rapids: Baker, 1992), 145–68.
14. Dietrich Bonhoeffer, *The Cost of Discipleship,* rev. ed. (New York: Macmillan, 1979), 99.

Walking with the Holy Spirit

Gonzalez notes that the basis for Christian spirituality is the Holy Spirit, the third person of the Trinity. One is spiritual because of the presence and indwelling of the Holy Spirit. A spiritual person, a spiritual teacher, is one in whom the Spirit of the Lord dwells.[15] A spirituality without the Holy Spirit is a scandal in Christian faith and in Christian teaching. Christian spirituality is a way of deepening the experience of God's active presence through the work of the Holy Spirit in one's own life, in the life of the church, and in the history of the world. Christian spirituality is about opening oneself to the healing power of the Spirit which enables persons to become whole and reconciled with themselves, with God, and with the world.[16] The world is God's creation and the object of God's love (John 3:16). The world is in need of teachers who give evidence of God's love by manifesting the distinct marks of Christian spirituality.

Marks of Christian Spirituality

Christian educators and leaders can both embrace and nurture the ten marks of Christian spirituality identified by the World Council study.[17]

Reconciling and integrative. A genuine spirituality is directed toward the wholeness of persons and communities. A danger exists in focusing on content or persons within Christian teaching to the exclusion of the wider community and society. Letty M. Russell speaks of this danger in relation to partnership.[18] In addition, teachers should work for the common good, submerging private agendas and seeking unity across the diversity of spiritual life that persons experience in each Christian faith community.[19] Teachers

15. González, *Mañana*, 158.
16. *Spiritual Formation*, 11.
17. Ibid., 13–16; I have drawn from this work and both elaborated upon and revised it in what follows.
18. See the discussion of partnership in chapter 2.
19. See the work of Habermas and Issler, *Teaching for Reconciliation*, for elaboration on the theme of reconciliation. A danger exists in Christian ministry of a rush to reconciliation that does not allow for exploring the causes and nature of conflict along with what is required for conversion or transformation.

must not impose their form of spirituality upon their students, but must offer it as a gift that honors the spiritual gifts of others.

Incarnational. A genuine spirituality addresses the here and now. In teaching this may require setting aside a plan when it is necessary to deal with pressing problems and issues that students may present. This approach does not succumb to the tyranny of the present, but represents an openness and a flexibility to allow the Holy Spirit to work in unexpected ways through teaching.

Rooted in Scripture and nourished by prayer. Christian education classes and events can provide times to share prayer concerns and to pray. It is also possible in some worship settings to uphold in prayer particular teachers and their general concerns, without breaching confidentiality. This can be done in pastoral prayers and regular prayer times during the week. The content of Scripture cannot be ignored as the key source for the Christian faith, especially in a time of biblical and theological illiteracy. Teachers need encouragement in their personal and group practice of prayer and Bible study.

Costly and self-giving. Christian spirituality confronts the reality of the cross of Christ in the world and in the life of many people who experience suffering and loss. The challenges of discipleship must be shared with teachers along with recognition of their acts of self-giving. Teacher recruitment that dismisses the costs of teaching must be avoided. The Christian faith confronts the scandal of particularity in the unique life and ministry of Jesus Christ. It also confronts the scandal of vulnerability as modeled in the lives of the *anawim*, and most fully in the life of Jesus himself. This confrontation applies to the various ministries of teaching as teachers seek to manifest the life of Christ in their lives with students.

Life giving and liberative. Like birthing and parenting, spiritual formation provides space for life to grow. It also encourages teachers to advocate for those concerns close to the heart of God. Christian teachers are to encourage choosing and affirming life as God's gift to humanity and the entire creation. Teachers are engaged in a spiritual conflict with powers and principalities opposed to God. They are called upon to withstand the forces that destroy life by enabling students to name those forces and to claim the resources of God's Spirit for daily living.

Rooted in community and centered around the eucharist, communion, or Lord's Supper. The eucharist is the banquet of God's reign and the center of worship. Teaching can be imaged as serving a feast or as setting a table at which all are welcome.[20] In relation to the eucharist, which refers to thanksgiving, a key question to ask is Do teachers attend corporate worship and participate around the Lord's table? If they are unable to regularly participate, one option may be to have a spiritual retreat for teachers. But some form of regular participation in worship is important for their spiritual nourishment. Teachers need regular times for renewal, sabbath, and refreshment. Teachers need significant times for fellowship with the entire Christian community. Teachers cannot share what they themselves do not possess. It is prudent to use strategies such as team teaching whereby teachers can rotate responsibilities.

Expressed in service and witness. Spirituality involves a commitment to action, to words and deeds. Teaching is active service and serves as a witness to God's continued teaching in the Christian community. The danger in many church settings is that of burnout, when times of service and times of sabbath and receptivity to the ministry of others do not balance. Leaders can advocate specified terms of service that allow for teachers themselves to be taught by others. In teaching we are taught, but teachers need the mutual ministry in the Christian church in order to effectively serve and witness.

Waiting for God's surprising initiatives. Teaching requires openness to God's mystery and surprises. Nurturing this receptivity may be fostered by asking a simple question of teachers: What is God doing in your life and teaching? This waiting is also nurtured through regular times of prayer that allow for silence and active listening to God. Teaching that so stresses activity may not nurture a needed receptivity to renewal by God's Spirit.

Unfolding the loving purposes of God on earth. This mark of Christian spirituality is inspired by the prayer that God's will be done on earth as it is in heaven. This mark signals the need to link the transcendent and the immanent dimensions of God through any ministry that includes teaching. Discerning this connection

20. Pazmiño, *Principles and Practices*, 120–22.

requires time and freedom to evaluate teaching in relation to its foundations in the Christian faith.

Open to the wider Christian church and the truths shared by other religious faiths. This requires of Christians an openness to the wider household of God or the other flock of the good Shepherd and to God's general revelation through common grace. This perspective avoids a spirituality captive to our own culture and the idols we too readily embrace in Christian churches. This openness avoids the arrogance of some Christians who refuse to see all truth as God's truth. In relation to Christian teachers, such an openness involves a risk along with a willingness to be challenged, including the challenge presented by ecumenical dialogue.

Nurturing these ten marks in teaching requires that teachers be filled with the Spirit and be open to grow. The ultimate purpose of the teaching ministry—namely, to glorify and enjoy God forever—must always be kept in focus. The ministry of teaching is a high calling and Christian teachers must discern the quality of their discipleship with Jesus Christ and the quality of their walk with the Holy Spirit so that the gospel may be lived in and out through their teaching. This is the basis for the authority of one's person and gifts in teaching. But the personal and practical question remains for the Christian teacher as to whether one has a gift for teaching. An implication of all that has been explored in this chapter is that a person serving as a Christian teacher has, in fact, a gift for teaching. This gift is recognized in the act of teaching by responding to needs in a particular ministry setting. The gift is God's, given for service and recognized by the church and the individual who serves.

Do You Have a Gift for Teaching?

Several insights can be shared as persons explore the question of having or not having a gift for teaching. Initially one must define the gift of teaching. Teaching in the biblical sense is *the process of sharing God's revelation along with the calling for personal and corporate decision and obedience.* It involves handing down the content of the Christian faith with implications for the public and private life of persons. Both Nehemiah 8:1–12 and Ephesians 4:11–13 describe the gift of teaching in

71

the faith community. This gift requires an ability to communicate content to and with others that results in their edification. Edification is important: "To each is given the manifestation of the Spirit for the common good" (1 Cor. 12:7).

Norman E. Harper observed that in one sense all Christians have the gift of teaching. Christian parents are called upon to teach their children by bringing them up in the discipline and instruction of the Lord (Eph. 6:4). All Christian persons have the responsibility to share with friends and/or family what they understand the Scriptures or Christian theology to be teaching. But the Scripture refers to teaching as a distinctive gift (Rom. 12:7; 1 Cor. 12:28: Eph. 4:11) that involves "an unusual and identifiable ability to understand the truth, conceptualize it in terms common to a large range of people, and explain it to them."[21] This gift is recognized by other Christians with whom one is serving.

As a spiritual gift, teaching is a gracious gift from God to persons for service, for the life of the Christian community (1 Pet. 4:10; 1 Cor 12:7). The gift is given by the Holy Spirit to the church for its edification, for the upbuilding of Christ's body. Any ability ignited and used by the Holy Spirit is a legitimate spiritual gift. All abilities and gifts are from God (1 Cor. 4:7; James 1:17–18). In one sense there are no native or natural abilities. But a spiritual gift is one especially given and activated by the Holy Spirit. The Holy Spirit redirects and uses natural endowments and abilities in God's service. A natural ability to teach does not become a spiritual gift until it is given to the Spirit for service. What is essential is a believing or an unbelieving use of gifts and abilities. A key question is Do we recognize our ability as a talent from God and in prayer and continued dedication do we commit it to God?[22]

Having defined the teaching gift in general terms, teachers can consider specific insights to discern their personal situation. First, all Christians must recognize that they have at least one spiritual gift. This is the teaching of the Scriptures in 1 Corinthians 12:1,

21. Norman E. Harper, *Making Disciples: The Challenge of Christian Education at the End of the 20th Century* (Memphis: Christian Studies Center, 1981), 135.

22. Howard A. Snyder, "Misunderstanding Spiritual Gifts," *Christianity Today* 18 (12 October 1973): 15–18.

11; Ephesians 4:7–8 ; and 1 Peter 4:10–11. The passage in 1 Peter is helpful to note:

> Like good stewards of the manifold grace of God, serve one another with whatever gift each of you has received. Whoever speaks must do so as one speaking the very words of God; whoever serves must do so with the strength that God supplies, so that God may be glorified in all things through Jesus Christ. To him belong the glory and the power forever and ever. Amen.

To each or to every Christian has been given a gift. An elaboration of this passage that explores being good stewards of God's grace helps to consider the gift of teaching.

Teaching is described elsewhere in Scripture as a spiritual gift (1 Cor. 12:28–31) listed third in order of God's appointment. But this gift requires a stewardship for teachers to serve others with what has been received from God. Truth from God's Word in its manifold expressions that has been made real to us in our lives must then be taught to others through the gift of teaching. The teacher must speak the very words of God. Consciously and intentionally teachers seek to enable students to be confronted (along with themselves first) by God and to encounter God speaking to them through the Scripture and in the person of Jesus Christ by the work of the Holy Spirit. Teaching requires working with a strength and an ability that are of God. Teachers are conscious of their own inability and incompetence and therefore are dependent upon God's resources (Rom. 8:32). The place of prayer and reliance upon the Holy Spirit is crucial in accessing God's resources. Finally, God must be glorified through Christ in the ministry of teaching. Teachers are called to view teaching as ministry to and with God as well as to and with others. As a Christian teacher, one is to direct persons to God and to encourage praise and adoration before their Creator. Thus the gift of teaching requires speaking for God and serving the faith community with the gifts and the strength that God provides. The ultimate end must always be in view, namely, the glory of God through Jesus Christ.

Second, those exploring the gift of teaching can pray that God will make their spiritual gifts known to them. It is important to realize that God delights to reveal God's will for humankind.

This promise is found in the wise saying recorded in Proverbs 3:5–6:

> Trust in the Lord with all your heart
> and do not rely on your own insight.
> In all your ways acknowledge him,
> and he will make straight your paths.

Trusting and acknowledging one's accountability to and reliance upon God places the question of one's gift in its proper perspective.

Third, persons exploring the gift of teaching should seek to exercise various gifts in the church as opportunity is provided. This requires taking on responsibility in the church or other ministry setting and asking for feedback and evaluation from those with whom one is teaching. This requires risking disclosure and discovery of one's gifts in the practice of educational ministry. The initial exploration may feel awkward and intimidating simply because it is a new experience.

Fourth, the prospective teacher should ask herself or himself Which of my gifts does God seem to bless and use in this particular ministry or setting? One must be honest in evaluating the results or fruits of one's teaching. These results may suggest the need to teach with an age group or in a setting other than one's current ministry. They also may suggest the need for further training.

Fifth, it is usually helpful to inquire of mature Christians who know you well, what your gifts might be and whether they include the gift of teaching. Those with more experience can often provide perspective and share wisdom about your ministry that is not immediately apparent or discernible. Be open to this feedback, but it may be necessary to hear from more than one other person. This additional input can serve to confirm or to question initial impressions that you or one other person hold.

Sixth, if one has received confirming feedback that one indeed may have a gift for teaching, new responsibilities are posed. One must seek to develop one's gifts in the power of the Holy Spirit. One must recognize that these gifts are from God and therefore the teacher must commit them to God as part of one's spiritual service. This is necessary to guard against the possibility of a false spiritual pride. Genuine pride celebrates the privilege of service, but false pride loses perspective on the giver of the gift, namely,

God, and compares one's possession of a gift with the gifts of others. The distinction of appropriate and genuine pride is suggested in Galatians 6:1–5:

> My friends, if anyone is detected in a transgression, you who have received the Spirit should restore such a one in a spirit of gentleness. Take care that you yourselves are not tempted. Bear one another's burdens, and in this way you will fulfill the law of Christ. For if those who are nothing think they are something, they deceive themselves. All must test their own work; then that work, rather than their neighbor's work, will become a cause for pride. For all must carry their own loads.

False pride is preoccupied with being better than others, whereas genuine pride considers one's own work in response to God's call. The person who is called by God to a teaching ministry and therefore gifted for such must seek out training and continuing education to develop that gift.

Confirmation of one's teaching gift corresponds with the possibility that one may not have this gift. If this is the case, persons must realize that they may have some other gifts of which they are not presently aware. Teaching may not be the gift one has received, but a host of other spiritual gifts are given to God's people and are essential for ministry.

Seventh and finally, a Christian teacher must be aware that she or he is ultimately accountable to God for the stewardship of her or his spiritual gifts. James 3:1 poses a challenge for teachers in relation to this accountability: "Not many of you should become teachers, my brothers and sisters, for you know that we who teach will be judged with greater strictness." A greater liability is laid upon those who are teachers and a greater responsibility. This responsibility is compensated for in the great joy experienced in being faithful to God's call and in using one's spiritual gifts for the edification of God's people and the extension of Christ's reign in the world. Chapter 4 will consider the authority of the teacher's experience as she or he seeks to be faithful to God's call to use one's gift.

But two questions can be posed for those considering the authority of one's person and teaching gift.[23] Should only Chris-

---

23. These questions are posed by Kevin E. Lawson.

tians with the gift of teaching teach in the church? At one level the answer to this first question is yes. But persons may not know about their teaching gift until they have actually taken the responsibility of teaching and sought the feedback of others, including those being taught. In this case the more important question to discern is whether one has been called to teach in a particular setting. Responding to the call is the first step in discerning the nature of one's teaching gift. If one is teaching and having some measure of positive response in meeting needs, then one can assume one has a teaching gift, even if only in beginning form. This gift requires the stewardship of the teacher within the larger faith community.

A second question is Are those with teaching gifts the only ones empowered and given authority to teach? Certainly pastors, elders, and deacons are called to teach and have authority in areas of their ministries; parents have a calling and an authority to teach their children. But the Scripture along with my ministry experience confirms the insight that those with teaching gifts are empowered and given authority to teach as a means by which to serve the Christian church and the world. Those with such gifts represent a wide diversity of teaching styles and approaches. They share a commitment to the common good of God's mission in the world and are empowered by the Holy Spirit.

4

Authority of One's Experience

Personal experience provides an incarnation of one's gifts (explored in chap. 3) and one's calling by God to teach in the faith community (explored in chaps. 2–3). Christian teachers possess authority on the basis of their experience with God and their identification with those in need. This was evidenced in the descriptions of the *anawim* (chap. 3). But in an age preoccupied only with the primacy of unexamined personal or communal experience, the grounding or foundation for that experience and its implicit authority must not be forgotten. Spiritual power and authority emerge from one's communion with God,[1] but the stress upon this communion can result in a tendency to uncritically validate all experiences. To guard against such a tendency, Christian teachers must be discerning of their own personal experiences and those of others. Spiritual experiences are validated by their connections to Scripture, the experiences of others in the faith

1. This is suggested by describing spiritual power as "being in communion with God" (p. 18 in the discussion of the definition of authority).

77

community, and personal reflection. These connections serve to confirm the work of the Holy Spirit in Christian teaching.

To assist such discernment, I will review from an integrative perspective what has been discussed in the first three chapters. Such a review corresponds with a model I occasionally have used in teaching. At the halfway point in a course I have conducted an evaluation that can make a difference in how the remainder of the course will be taught. Evaluation can provide reminders of what is essential and foundational to the experience of students as well as the teacher.[2]

Review

To explore authoritative education, teachers are assisted by having a good theory by which to assess their practice and experience. A good theory, which in the case of Christian teaching draws upon theology, can provide perspective on the complexity of teaching and on evaluating what has or has not been accomplished. One underlying form that I have identified for teaching is the educational trinity. The educational trinity consists of the three elements of content, persons, and context that need to be balanced throughout the educational process. In fact, education in general can be defined as the process of sharing content with persons in the context of their community and society.[3] Content in Christian teaching includes an intellectual, emotional, and active response to God's revelation, in particular the gospel of grace and redemption in Jesus Christ.

How does the educational trinity relate to the experience of teaching? First, teaching that focuses primarily upon content stresses the logical order of the material shared, the experience of the mind. In Christian teaching a particular type of logic, theology, is central. Theology is informed by the revelation of God and centers upon God. In theology God's revelation is systematically or logically discussed.

2. For a more detailed discussion of educational evaluation, see Robert W. Pazmiño, *Principles and Practices of Christian Education: An Evangelical Perspective* (Grand Rapids: Baker, 1992), chap. 6, "Educational Evaluation," 145–68.
    3. For further discussion of the educational trinity see Pazmiño, *Principles and Practices*, 10, 23–24, 45, 65, 158–63.

Second, teaching that focuses primarily upon the context stresses the sociological or cultural order of the material shared, the experience in a particular community or society. The experience stressed can be actual or hypothetical. In Christian teaching a particular community is central, namely, the church both gathered and scattered in the world (see chap. 2).

Third, teaching that focuses primarily upon persons stresses the psychological or existential order of the material shared, the experience of individual persons in the world. In Christian teaching particular persons are central, namely, those who are or are considering being disciples of Jesus Christ. This focus does not exclude genuine love and respect for those outside the Christian faith, for they are also created in God's image. It does not exclude the possibility of interfaith dialogue and interaction (the theme of chap. 6). In Christian teaching we encourage Christian persons to work for the good of all persons in the world. The special emphasis is upon Christian persons (Gal. 6:10): "So then, whenever we have opportunity, let us work for the good of all, and especially for those of the family of faith." The focus upon Christian persons includes nurturing the relationships that Christians have with the persons of the Trinity (discussed in chap. 1).

How does this perspective of the educational trinity relate to what has been considered in the first three chapters of this work, and how does it relate to the authority of one's experience in teaching?

Chapter 1 considered the theological foundation of God's authority as essential for teaching with authority. It is interesting to note that P. T. Forsyth historically argued that the cross of Jesus Christ is the final seat of authority for Christians.[4] In a similar vein, Ronald Cram currently argues that the praxis of teaching and learning may be seen as a faithful response to God's love revealed in the cross. Therefore, "Christian education is inherently based on the Trinity, revealed in the cross of Golgotha."[5] God's

4. P. T. Forsyth, "The Cross as the Final Seat of Authority," *Contemporary Review* 76 (October 1899): 589–609.
5. Ronald H. Cram, "Christian Education in Theological Education," *Religious Education* 87 (Summer 1992): 333–35. It is possible to propose that the two organizing principles I suggest in *Principles and Practices*, namely, conversion and connection, can be better integrated with what Cram identifies as the central organizing principle for Christian education, the cross of Christ.

authority and call must ground the content and the experience of the Christian teacher. The Christian teacher must start with God and her or his relationship with God made most explicit in Christ's cross. In Christian teaching, personal experience without this foundational content is blind, lacks authority, and leads to fragmentation.[6] Therefore a discussion of authority in teaching must develop from considering the following elements or loci: God as Trinity, the fontal authority; Jesus Christ as God's fullest revelation for humanity and the mediator between God and humanity in relation to authority; theological authority as mediate authority that centers sequentially upon the Scriptures, church traditions, and human experience. This foundation is indispensable to exploring the question of authority in Christian teaching.

Chapter 2 continued the discussion of theological concerns, but included communal and sociological insights. This chapter focused upon the context of Christian teaching, the church and its exercise of institutional or communal authority. The church is a community of faith that takes on sociological significance in relation to various educational structures that exist in modern life. These other educational structures include the family, the community, the economy, the media, the school, and the body politic.[7] Chapter 2 illustrated the need to relate theological understandings to communal and sociological realities. In theology the study of the church and its polity or ecclesiology provides the essential connection. The experience of Christian teaching must be related to the mission and purposes of the church. That mission includes the tasks of proclamation, community, service, advocacy, and worship.[8] Christian teaching must help persons relate their lives to the ongoing mission of the church and to their part in that greater mission. Knowing and appreciating the what

6. Lois E. LeBar observed that Christian content without experience is empty and that experience without content is blind; Lois E. LeBar, "Curriculum," in *An Introduction to Evangelical Christian Education*, ed. J. Edward Hakes (Chicago: Moody, 1964), 89.

7. For a description of the educational impact of these structures see Pazmiño, *Principles and Practices of Christian Education*, chap. 3, "Educational Structures," 59–90.

8. I discuss these five tasks of proclamation, community, service, advocacy, and worship as constituting another underlying form of Christian teaching, the five-task model. See ibid., 10, 45–56, 94–95, 163–67.

and why of Christian teaching in relation to the mission of the church provides an indispensable perspective for the teacher. The church and its mission provides the context in which the teacher's authority is legitimated and exercised.

Chapter 3 continued the interest and concern with understanding the nature and mission of the church, but with a different focus: how teachers use the gifts they have received for the common good within the faith community. The discussion of spirituality focused upon the person of the teacher and her or his discipleship with Jesus and walk with the Spirit. The authority of the teacher's person and gifts is contingent upon the faithfulness of one's discipleship and the ever-present grace of God. God's grace is crucial, because persons are creatures of God and their abilities to teach are gifts that God has graced upon humanity. Teachers are responsible for the stewardship of these gifts within the faith community. Teachers also recognize ways in which their discipleship and walk have not been faithful. In these areas, teachers rely upon God's grace for forgiveness, cleansing, and power to live differently. This is the message of the gospel and the cross of Christ applied to human experience. The authority of the teacher's person and gifts are intimately connected with one's relationship to God the source of all gifts (James 1:17), to Jesus Christ the unspeakable gift (2 Cor. 9:15; Rom. 8:32), and to the Holy Spirit, the giver of gifts to the church (1 Cor. 12:4–11).

This review leads us to consider the authority of the teacher's experience in relation to the broader perspective provided by the educational trinity. Without this perspective, the teacher's experience can lose its moorings and result in a shipwreck in teaching the Christian faith. What then of experience if content without experience is empty?

The Place of Experience

A popular proverb captures the dilemma of exerience in teaching: "Experience is the best teacher, but is the school of the fool." Experience is to be valued, but only in relation to other factors in Christian teaching. The experience of God is essential to Christian life, but not all claims to such experience are true, good, and valuable for teaching. Experience must be balanced with opportunities for reflection that relate the experiences to Christian content, to Christian theology as derived from a study of the Scriptures. Personal experience must also be balanced with feedback and evaluation from others both within and without the Christian community. Experience must be seen as multidimensional and inclusive of reason, emotion, and will. Experience also includes historical, sociological, political, economic, cultural, familial, and personal experiences. For the Christian teacher, experience must be related to life in God, in Jesus Christ, and in the Holy Spirit for it to be authoritative in Christian teaching. If it is not, the illumination attributed to experience can result in illusion, and the discernment attributed to experience can result in delusion. In Christian faith all good theology connects with experience, but all experience is not necessarily theologically grounded and appropriate for teaching. What makes the difference?

The place of experience in authoritative teaching is directly related to the narrative description of experience. Stephen Crites argued for the essential narrative quality of all experience itself.[9] Susanne Johnson observes that Christians are shaped by three basic texts of story: life story, cultural story, and Christian story. Teaching is that ministry in the church's work that seeks to bring these three stories into conversation.[10] The life story or experience of the teacher takes on authority at the point of its connection with the Christian and the cultural stories. In a similar perspective, Les L. Steele names three types of narrative that are useful for theology: canonical or biblical story, faith community story, and life story. Life story is the story of one's own faith and life, and the task of narrative theology is to both tell and critique these stories.[11] Only from a telling and critiquing that explores the correlation of the teacher's experience and story with both the Christian and the church's stories can authority emerge.

9. Stephen Crites, "The Narrative Quality of Experience," *Journal of the American Academy of Religion* 39 (September 1971): 291–311.
10. Susanne Johnson, *Christian Spiritual Formation in the Church and Classroom* (Nashville: Abingdon, 1989), 90.
11. See Gabriel Fackre, "Narrative Theology: An Overview," *Interpretation* 37 (October 1983): 360, and Les L. Steele, *On the Way: A Practical Theology of Christian Formation* (Grand Rapids: Baker, 1990), 16.

The three stories that both Johnson and Steele identify have a direct relationship with the definition of education that I proposed: education is the sharing of content with persons in the context of their community and society. A sensitivity to persons in Christian education requires attention to their personal or life stories. A sensitivity to the context of the community and society in Christian education requires attention to the cultural or faith community story. A sensitivity to content in Christian education requires attention to the Christian or the biblical story. *All three stories or all three educational elements must be attended to in integrating personal experience in Christian teaching.*

Personal experience must be related to one's relationships in the faith community. Confirmation and correction of personal experience come through dialogue and interaction with Christian sisters and brothers who provide both affirmation and critique. In a critical age, it is essential to allow for genuine affirmation and the support of others. Too often critique is used to dismiss any contributions that others can make. But the place of constructive criticism is also to be recognized in the Christian ministry of teaching.

The late Robert A. Cook, former president of Kings College, shared practical advice: If criticism is true then one should heed it; if it is not true, then one should ignore it and go on. The ministry of teaching involves criticism and a realization that one cannot please everyone. Therefore the Christian teacher should strive to please God and learn to accept human criticism. Paul's description of his ministry in Thessalonica makes this explicit (1 Thess. 2). God can speak to us through the criticism of others, and God may also be calling us to persevere in the midst of opposition.

The issue of the authority of experience can be related to the question as to whether teachers are born or made. If teachers are born teachers, experience is not crucial as a basis for authority. But if teachers are made, experience *is* crucial for authority. I do not perceive the situation as being either/or, but rather both/and. Christian teachers are born persons whose existence is dependent upon the grace and love of God. They are born with various abilities and skills that may include an orientation toward those required for teaching. In addition, Christian teachers are born anew by the Spirit of God and are equipped for spiritual ministry by virtue of the gifts endowed upon the Christian church (1 Cor. 12:7–11). Thus, Christian teachers are born. But Christian teachers are also being made by the continuing process of sanctification in which the teacher is called to be increasingly conformed to the image of Christ by the work of the Spirit within the faith community and the world. Christian teachers are being made in their formative experiences that serve as a basis for their sharing not only the content of their teaching, but themselves as well.

A mystery is implied in the fact that God is at work in teachers while they are responsible for their response to God through their teaching. Philippians 2:12b–13 describes this dynamic in relation to salvation that has implications for a teaching ministry: "work out your own salvation with fear and trembling; for it is God who is at work in you, enabling you both to will and to work for his good pleasure." The response to God includes training, discipline, diligence, and action motivated by love. A Christian teacher must ask herself or himself the following questions that serve to evaluate one's experience and validate one's authority: Am I a teacher called and gifted by God? Am I an effective teacher? Am I an increasingly effective teacher? Beyond the consideration of discerning gifts (chap. 3), the teacher explores the matter of one's duty. The teaching of Luke 17:7–10 suggests that the duty of Christian teachers is to serve Christ as our Lord. Our duty in service is to seek to be an increasingly effective teacher by the grace and strength of God. Such is the challenge that makes a teaching experience both exciting and frustrating. Excitement comes through being used by God and contributing to the lives of others. Frustration is experienced in addressing the costs of service and the risks of teaching itself. (One hopes the experience of teaching is more encouraging than discouraging). The costs of teaching support Forsyth's observation that the cross is the final seat of authority in Christian ministry. But beyond the cross lies the resurrection as God works through human limitations to bring new life. The place of experience in Christian teaching has been recently explored in relation to praxis ways of knowing and the advocacy of action-reflection models for teaching.

An Excursus: The Current Interest in Praxis

In the effort to recognize the essential place of experience in life, Christian educators in recent work have advocated consideration of praxis, the dynamic interaction of action and reflection (i.e., experience and reflection upon that experience). Using personal and corporate experience as the point of entry into teaching has been advocated as an alternative to approaches that begin with considerations of content.[12] Relying on content as the entry point of teaching may mean that experience is never adequately considered; beginning with experience or action avoids this pitfall. An alternative dynamic follows that fosters a dialogue between action or experience and reflection. The teacher expects that reflection will result in personal and corporate action. What is generally assumed in this perspective is that reflection is not itself an action. But it is possible to see reflection as an action of the mind, soul, and body. Max Stackhouse observes that praxis thought derives from the work of Aristotle and Plato:

> In classical philosophy, *praxis* was understood to be one of the three basic ways of knowing, living, and being in the world. It stands distinct from, but in complementary relationship to, both *poesis* and *theoria*. *Poesis* involves imaginative creation or representation of evocative images. It includes the kind of awareness and orientation to life that can be discovered by aesthetic and kinesthetic experience. *Theoria* involves observation, reporting, interpretation, and critical evaluation. It thus includes all that can be known by analysis, systematic study, reflection, and contemplation. The central issues of *theoria* are less aesthetic or kinesthetic than ontological, metaphysical, and epistemic. In contrast to these, *praxis* involves intentional, practical engagement whereby people seek to do something for the common good. However, the kind of life and world orientation that derives from *praxis* is not unrelated to *poesis* or *theoria*. . . . *Praxis*, in short, has become the technical term for the "action/reflection"

12. See the work of Thomas H. Groome, *Sharing Faith: A Comprehensive Approach to Religious Education and Pastoral Ministry: The Way of Shared Praxis* (San Francisco: Harper San Francisco, 1991). Groome advocates the place of shared praxis that moves beyond classical distinctions to realize a partnership of theoria, praxis, and poesis proposed by Aristotle.

mode of teaching and learning, one that does not focus primarily on either speculative theory or aesthetic expression, but accepts these as possible resources for action.[13]

The value of praxis approaches can be affirmed in relation to what Brazilian educator Paulo Freire observed. Freire points out two dangers in teaching. One danger is mere activism that emphasizes learning by doing or experience without a corresponding concern for thought and reflection. The other danger is mere verbalism that stresses thought, reflection, and speech that are divorced from practical implications or the realities of life.[14] Praxis is offered as an alternative.

The primary commitment to praxis as embodying the most faithful way to include experience in teaching can be questioned. The discernment of orthopraxis, true and just praxis, requires at some point reference to theoria and poesis. The consideration of action and experience cannot be discounted, but it must be held in relation to what Samuel Solivan has identified as orthodoxy (right and true belief or theoria) and orthopathos (right and true passion that can be expressed in poesis).[15] The appeal to praxis and orthopraxis in teaching and learning must be heard in relation to the content or theoria that grounds its perspective. In Christian teaching, grounding is found primarily in theology that enables persons to make sense of their experience and to relate that personal experience to the faith community and the wider society. As an alternative to praxis-based epistemology, an ecclesial epistemology can be proposed to ground theology:

> In simple terms this means that we can know more and better as a group than we can as individuals. The very diversity of viewpoints is more likely to elicit a better understanding than is the internal consistency of a single viewpoint. (As Emerson, I be-

13. Max L. Stackhouse, *Apologia: Contextualization, Globalization, and Mission in Theological Education* (Grand Rapids: Eerdmans, 1988), 84–85.

14. Paulo Freire, *Pedagogy of the Oppressed*, trans. Myra Bergman Ramos (New York: Seabury, 1970), 75–76. For a detailed discussion of Freire's work see Daniel S. Schipani, *Religious Education Encounters Liberation Theology* (Birmingham, Ala.: Religious Education Press, 1988).

15. See Samuel Solivan, "Orthopathos: Interlocutor between Orthodoxy and Praxis," *Andover Newton Review* 1 (Winter 1990): 19–25.

lieve, observed, "consistency is the hobgoblin of little minds.")
Irenaeus observed that "All truth is Christian," and by this he
meant not a religious take-over-bid, but the genuine openness of
the faith to all that we can know. It is in the exchange of ideas
and values that occur in discussion and debate that we continue
on the way to God.[16]

An ecclesial epistemology enables Christians to gain the insights
offered from theoria, poesis, and praxis without opting for one
way of knowing or one viewpoint as dominant. But a practical
question remains and must be addressed: What does theology
teach us about the value of experience, particularly in relation to
teaching?

The Value of Experience

The value of experience can be seen in biblical examples.[17] In
Luke 24, as the two disciples encountered the risen Christ on the
road to Emmaus, Jesus asked the disciples questions. Why did he
do this and not directly share what he knew? Jesus validated the
experience of these disciples because he could not effectively
teach them until he had first heard their stories and their perspectives on the prophecies about him. Later in this same chapter of
Luke Jesus appeared to his disciples in Jerusalem as they gathered behind closed doors. He did not initially emphasize content,
even though the reality of the resurrection was crucial to their
understanding of what God had accomplished. Sharing personal
experience or story was crucial here as well. Jesus used their perception of seeing a ghost as the entry point for his teaching. Jesus
related his resurrected presence to all five of the human senses
before he disclosed propositional truth to his followers. These
examples serve to indicate the value of experience in the Jesus'
teaching ministry and suggest its value in Christian teaching
today.

16. Meredith B. Handspicker, "Being on the Way: Theological Education
and the Question of Truth," occasional paper, January 1993, presented at Andover Newton Theological School, Newton Centre, Massachusetts, 4.
17. Ronald Habermas shared these insights in responding to an initial draft
of this work.

Gabriel Fackre observes that experience in the setting of the world provides Christians with signs or aids to illumine their faith and life. Fackre advocates understanding authority with the Bible as its source, Christ as its center, and the gospel as its substance. But he also identifies the importance of the church as the resource for understanding the gospel and the world as the setting in which Christians live and discern signs. These signs are held in relation to both the tradition that serves as a guide for the church (the resource for authority) and the gospel that serves as substance encountered in the Bible (the source of authority): "In the general setting of authority are to be found 'signs' of special significance. These are the points in human experience in which thinking approaches 'the true,' doing 'the good,' and feeling 'the beautiful.' As such they are of help in the statement of Christian teaching; aid is to setting as guide is to resource and substance to source."[18] The gospel and the tradition both hold priority over the place of these signs, but the signs nevertheless are important to consider. In one sense, personal experience is our daily reality and we must wrestle with it to make sense of life.

Faith Experience and Its Verification

Forsyth observed that our personal experience is verified by a variety of factors: its repetition, its continuity over time, and its external reference for individuals. Personal experience is also verified by its continuous and repeated relationship with the experience of other people. For Christians these other people include those in the Scripture and in the faith community, the church. An additional factor is the relationship of experience to conviction and life commitment. Conviction and commitment provide additional grounding. But Forsyth contends that

> the chief guarantee of the value of experience is not given by its actual universality, by its popularity, but by its content. . . . It is the content that turns psychology into theology, thought into revelation, and experience to faith. . . . Faith is a religious expe-

18. Gabriel Fackre, *The Christian Story: A Pastoral Systematics*, vol. 2, *Authority: Scripture in the Church for the World* (Grand Rapids: Eerdmans, 1987), 52–53.

rience, but religious experience is not faith. Faith is the gift and creation of God. . . . the experience of an active God creates faith, an approaching, revealing, recreating God, on one side, and the act of surrender on our side which replies. . . . It is the content of the experience that extends it from mere experience to a living and reliant faith.[19]

Therefore the value of experience in Christian life and teaching must be seen in relation to faith, in relation to the content of the Christian faith that persons encounter and embrace in their lives. The gospel, in the words of Justo González, is to be both lived in and lived out in the sense of making the faith the foundation of life, action, and structure.[20] The value and authority of the Christian teacher's experience is that teacher's faith and its expression in life. Forsyth's insights are again helpful:

If you claim the right to challenge the validity of my experience, you must do it on the ground of some experience surer, deeper, getting nearer moral reality than mine. What is it? Does the last criterion lie in sense, or even in thought? Is it not in conscience? If life at its center is moral, then the supreme certainty lies there. It must be associated, not with a feeling nor with a philosophic process, but with the last moral experience of life, which we find to be a life morally changed from the center and forever. To challenge that means rationalism, intellectualism, and the merest theosophy. Do not forget that philosophy is but a method, while faith, which is at the root of theology, presents us with a datum, a new reality.[21]

The reality of faith in God is the experience that Christian teachers can share. Their faith experience is interpreted in terms of the content of faith. That content provides a grounding upon which students can build and explore their own faith. Having experienced the truth of the gospel by faith, Paul the great teacher of the church was able to teach with zest and power. The lack of genu-

19. P. T. Forsyth, *The Principle of Authority in Relation to Certainty, Sanctity and Society: An Essay in the Philosophy of Experiential Religion*, 2d ed. (London: Independent, 1952), 24–30.

20. Justo L. González, *Mañana: Christian Theology from a Hispanic Perspective* (Nashville: Abingdon, 1990), 157.

21. Forsyth, *Gospel and Authority*, 67–68.

ine faith experience with God results in empty Christian teaching. What more can be said about the experience of faith?

The Dimensions of Faith

Faith is a gift of God's grace to humanity. Faith can be viewed as including the dimensions of *notitia* (intellectual affirmation), *assensus* (affective affirmation), and *fiducia* (intentional affirmation) as persons respond to God's activities and revelation in Jesus Christ. Acts 2:37 describes the integration of these three dimensions of faith: "Now when they heard [*notitia*] this [the gospel], they were cut to the heart [*assensus*] and said to Peter and to the other disciples, 'Brothers, what should we do [*fiducia*]?'" Thomas H. Groome expands upon these traditional dimensions in his description of lived Christian faith He first identifies a cognitive/mental dimension, a believing activity that reflects conviction and decision. He then names an affective/relational dimension, trusting in one's relationship with God in Jesus; this trust is nurtured within a Christian faith community and shapes one's relationship with all humanity. Thirdly, Groome identifies a behavioral/obediential dimension, doing God's will in the world.[22] Such activities serve as faith signs.

Faith Signs

The experience of faith in God as it is lived out calls for a response of the total person as suggested in the great commandment: to love the Lord our God with all of our heart, soul, mind, and strength and to love our neighbor as ourselves (Mark 12:30–31). Groome's behavioral/obediential dimension to Christian faith connects with what the apostle Paul suggests in Ephesians 2:8–10: "For by grace you have been saved through faith, and this is not your own doing; it is the gift of God—not the result of works, so that no one may boast. For we are what he has made us, created in Christ Jesus for good works, which God prepared beforehand to be our way of life." The importance of seeing the relationship among grace, faith, works and authority is discussed by Forsyth:

22. Groome, *Sharing Faith*, 18–20.

Christ comes full of grace and truth, but with the grace uppermost and always central. Grace represents the fixed, fontal, authoritative, evangelical element; truth, the element free, adjustable, and catholic. The one appeals to our personal life-conviction, the other to our scientific judgment. We own the authority of grace by impression and not perception, by conviction and not observation, by life and not by thought. It is in personal relation with us. It is the authority in it that breeds the knowledge, the science, the theology. It is not the knowledge that is the ground of the authority; it is the authority that is the ground of knowledge (though, of course, in the empirical order of time, the knowledge may come first). There is assent as well as trust. But the *fiducia* precedes the *assensus*, and produces it freely. The freedom that is worth most to Christian theology is not free thought but a free soul. It is not cosmic and rational, but ethical, vital, evangelical. It is not freedom of the world's harmony, but freedom of Christ's reconciliation, and free and freeing grace.[23]

The New Testament Book of James also stresses the connection between faith and works as an expression of God's grace. The experience of faith implies a predisposition to act in ways consistent with that faith. José Miguez Bonino has said that the goal of sharing the Christian faith is to elicit not only knowing in a cognitive sense, but also faithful obedience to the will of God.[24] Therefore the Christian teacher's works or actions provide the first faith sign or aid, to use Fackre's terms, for students in exploring faith. These faith signs provide a possible basis for authority to validate or verify that which is being shared.

A second faith sign is the nature of the relationships and affections that the teacher demonstrates in her or his life. These relationships and affections or loves may affirm or deny the gospel of Jesus Christ. The teacher discloses the order of loves that guide her or his life through teaching, and this disclosure influences the lives of students in ways more implicit than explicit. The place of passion and enthusiasm are to be affirmed in teaching. But a warning must be sounded in relation to the cultural wisdom of following one's bliss or passion. One's bliss or passion may lead

23. Forsyth, *Gospel and Authority*, 138–39.
24. José Miguez Bonino, *Doing Theology in a Revolutionary Situation* (Philadelphia: Fortress, 1975), 87.

to illusion or delusion. The Christian challenge is to follow God's bliss and passion (Ps. 37:3–4):

> Trust in the LORD, and do good;
>   so you will live in the land, and enjoy security.
> Take delight in the LORD,
>   and he will give you the desires of your heart.

Delight in God enables one to identify and embrace those true, good, and just passions or desires of the heart. Delight in God empowers one to pursue those desires that fulfill God's purposes for humanity and all of creation. Authoritative experience is genuine experience with God that is confirmed by the Holy Spirit through the Scriptures, the testimony of the faith community past and present, and personal reflection.

A third faith sign is the quality of the intellectual life and belief that the teacher models. This quality is a reflection of the commandment to love God with all of our mind (see chap. 5). These three faith signs of works, trusting relationships, and beliefs in the teacher's experience hold the potential for affecting the lives of students in transformative ways by the grace of God. But no guarantee exists that the authority of the shared experience based upon these faith signs will be received or effective. In one sense this authority must be earned over time and confirmed through the diligent efforts of the teacher and the gracious work of God in the lives of those called to teach and to be taught.

Authoritative teaching requires of teachers a continual process of communication and evaluation with others in the Christian church. In evaluation the potential exists for both affirmation and critique in relation to one's experience as a teacher and the experience of students with whom one is teaching. The place of both affirmation and critique is embodied in biblical faith that describes weal and woe as elements in God's covenant with humanity and creation. Faithful communication and evaluation are signs of effective teaching.

The experience of teaching can also be explored in terms of both Christian tradition and transformation. In fact, Mary C. Boys defines religious education in terms of both these aspects of Christian life: "Religious education is the making accessible of the traditions of the religious community and the making manifest of the intrinsic connection between traditions and transformation."[25] Traditions provide for structure and continuity in the Christian community. Teachers are called upon to effectively share these traditions with current and future generations. Transformation provides for change and new life in the Christian community that God graciously offers as persons experience the true and living God in Jesus Christ. Teachers are called upon to nurture the possibility for transformation in the lives of their students, in the faith community, and in the wider community and society.

C. S. Lewis observed, in relation to both life in general and Christian life, that mere change is not growth. Rather growth is the combination or synthesis of change and continuity, and where there is no continuity, there is no growth. Teachers are gatekeepers for the Christian community in relation to the ebb and flow of the tides of continuity and change. In the process of fulfilling God's call to stand at the gate, the hope and prayer is that teachers will contribute to the faith development of the Christian church and of those called to be their students. To the extent that they fulfill this call their experience can be authoritative.

Fostering Faith Development

The authority of the Christian teacher's experience, as has been suggested, must focus upon faith in Jesus Christ. Effective teaching nurtures faith in the lives of those being taught. Teachers must consider the faith development of those they teach. John H. Westerhoff provides a practical description of four faith styles across the lifespan that compares faith to the growth rings of a tree. As new styles or rings are added, the old rings are retained.[26]

The first style is experienced faith, in which children experience the faith of significant caregivers. Children learn to trust and have confidence in others, themselves, and God as a result of assimilating faith from faithful others. The authority of teachers'

25. Mary C. Boys, *Educating in Faith: Maps and Visions* (San Francisco: Harper and Row, 1989), 193.

26. For a description of these four styles of faith, see John H. Westerhoff III, *Will Our Children Have Faith?* (New York: Seabury, 1976), 89–91; and John H. Westerhoff, *Bringing Up Children in the Christian Faith* (Minneapolis: Winston, 1980), 25–27. Westerhoff's descriptions are drawn upon in what follows.

experience for those in infancy and early childhood is directly related to their trustworthiness and faithfulness in caring for the emerging generation.

The second style of faith is affiliative faith, which typifies middle and later childhood. Children with this style have a sense of belonging to a self-conscious and caring community. Persons with this style have a faith that seeks to belong and to be cared for by a community of faithing people. Identity in a community that provides for a sense of authority and nurtures positive affections is crucial. The authority of teachers' experience for persons with this style directly relates to the ability to welcome others and to form a sense of connection and community. It also relates to the ability to share those stories, perspectives, and values that characterize the Christian community and shape Christian identity.

Searching or struggling faith is the third style. Persons with this style are most typically youth and young adults who encounter a time of critical reflection and questioning of their faith and that of their family and community of origin. Doubt, experimentation, testing, and the exploration of commitment typify this style. Teachers' experience can be authoritative if teachers model openness and a willingness to question. The teacher who loves and accepts persons in the midst of their search will serve as an authority who can mentor or guide others.

Westerhoff's fourth style is owned faith, in which people freely choose to covenant with God. This faith style attempts to bring together professed faith with lifestyle and actions. Owned faith involves embracing one's conversion and affiliation with the Christian faith and a willingness to witness through words and deeds. The authority of the teachers' experience in the case of owned faith relates to evidence of both integrity and the operation of God's grace in their lives. Authentic disciples of Jesus the Christ are able to share that which they own, or better stated, are able to share what they have received from God, the gift of faith.

Beyond the four styles of faith suggested by Westerhoff, the work of V. Bailey Gillespie explored seven models of faith experience across the lifespan: borrowed faith in early childhood, reflected faith in middle childhood, personalized faith in early adolescence, established faith in later youth, reordered faith in young adults, reflective faith in middle adults, and resolute faith in older adults.[27] Gillespie's descriptions elaborate on Wester-hoff's styles and suggest entry points for teaching persons at different points in the life cycle.

The emphasis of this chapter upon the authority of experience (and in particular the experience of faith) must be balanced with the authority of reason in relation to expertise and study (chap. 5). Faith and reason can complement each other in authoritative Christian teaching. Faith experience can serve to foster expertise if reflection and study are also engaged in the practice of teaching.

Conclusion

Addison Leitch, a former professor of theology at Gordon Divinity School, observed that it is appropriate for persons to discuss personal experience because it is the only experience persons have. This chapter has explored how experience can be drawn upon in authoritative teaching. The discernment of experience is critical in relation to the touchstones of authority outlined in the first three chapters of this work. Without clarity in relation to fontal, mediate, theological, and institutional authority, the appeal to experience too often has led not to clarity but to confusion. Conversely, the lack of genuine experience with God has bankrupted Christian teaching. The experience of individuals or groups of persons in particular contexts must be examined in relation to the perennial content of the Christian faith and the foundations upon which Christian teaching emerges. The essential foundation is in Jesus Christ, the very Son of God. Dialogue that wrestles with Christian foundations is both the privilege and the responsibility of each generation of Christian teachers as they strive to be faithful to treasure of the gospel they hold in the

27. V. Bailey Gillespie, *The Experience of Faith* (Birmingham, Ala.: Religious Education Press, 1988), 79–84. Gillespie points out that "at times faith experiences are primarily cognitive. At other times they are primarily affective and personal. Furthermore, the experience of faith takes on the form of open commitment or casual consensus. It can be felt in open, creative ways, or it can be more withdrawn, more intellectual, and ideological. But during the life cycle there are characteristics of that faith that may focus our nurture and action as a religious community in a productive way" (84). One form of that nurture and action is teaching.

earthen vessels of their humanity. The faith experience with God provides the signs that Fackre named and serves to incarnate the eternal truths Christians seek to pass on to present and succeeding generations. Experience provides the color to what otherwise would be a drab landscape in teaching.

5

Authority of One's Expertise and Study

Chapter 4 explored the place of experience in authoritative teaching and the importance of faith experience with God. The exercise of expertise, study, reflection, and reason provide for the ordering of experience that is necessary to discern meaning in human life and the Christian life. The distinctive expertise that characterizes teaching is the use of reflection and reason. Teachers are qualified to address areas of educational content on the basis of their study. Teachers must ask themselves: Is my experience and the meaning derived from it warranted, and on what basis is it warranted? The search for warrants for our experience has led persons to ground their experience in recognized knowledge and/or revealed knowledge in the case of the Christian faith. But in this search it is essential that we recognize the limitations of our knowledge: "For now we see in a mirror, dimly, but then we will see face to face. Now I know only in part; then I will know fully, even as I have been fully known" (1 Cor. 13:12). In this life we know only in part and must rely upon the foundation of God's grace and revelation. We are fully known by God and therefore must rely upon God's perspective of the human situation and our experience to make sense of life. The sense and meaning we strive to make is always held with modesty and mystery, for we recognize our partial knowledge that awaits God's consummation. With our partial knowledge, we are always challenged to continue to study and learn from others.

While recognizing the limitations of our meaning making, we nevertheless strive to discern the truth and to rely upon the authority of expertise and study in our search for truth. The Scriptures suggest the importance of loving God with our minds (Matt. 22:37), and the apostle Paul encouraged believers to have the same mind that was in Jesus Christ (Phil. 2:5). Paul provides an expansive description of all that Christians should think about:

> Finally, beloved, whatever is true, whatever is honorable, whatever is just, whatever is pure, whatever is pleasing, whatever is commendable, if there is any excellence and if there is anything worthy of praise, think about these things. Keep on doing the things that you have learned and received and heard and seen in me, and the God of peace will be with you. [Phil. 4:8–9]

The thinking described here is connected thinking that links with what is modeled and lived out. But it is still thinking on a comprehensive scale. The Scriptures also call for a renewed mind (Rom. 12:2) that is ready and active in response to God's revelation. The work of a renewed mind includes the discipline of study.

In study we search out basic assumptions and principles. In this study we are engaged in open-ended inquiry that allows for ever-new light and truth to be discerned from God's Word. We recognize the need to always be reformed in our thinking and judging among a host of options presented to persons in a postmodern world. We recognize the need to be in dialogue with many others if our reflection is not only to sustain our private world, but also to address our public world that includes the Christian church and the wider society. This dialogue with others includes various communities of discourse that have historically sought after truth and have taught truths to succeeding generations. These communities may transcend traditional academic guilds to include community groups that embody wisdom in their way of life. Their wisdom is named as common sense and is not identified as philosophy or written in books such as this work you are reading. Honoring the voices of those historically excluded, like the *anawim*, is essential for those who would teach in transformative ways and gain expertise that transcends the ordinary. Christian teaching implies an openness to the extraordinary and to the place of mystery and awe that surrounds God, who is our teacher for eternity. But our God has created persons with minds that must be exercised in the tasks of living, learning, and teaching with authority.

The identification of expertise assumes that certain persons have had the opportunity to study or to reflect upon life and their experience and that of others. With this opportunity comes the responsibility to share with others what one has gained and to do so with integrity. This sharing takes the form of teaching, but is not limited to formal settings of education. Much can be shared and learned from nonformal and informal settings in which persons spontaneously inquire about the nature and the quality of life.[1] One common element across the various educational settings is that of reflection; Jackson W. Carroll proposes that authority in ministry, and I would add teaching, can be seen as the exercise of reflective leadership.[2] In Christian faith, teaching itself is a ministry.

Reflection

In his model of reflective leadership in ministry Carroll identifies both background and foreground elements that require

---

1. See Robert W. Pazmiño, *Principles and Practices of Christian Education: An Evangelical Perspective* (Grand Rapids: Baker, 1992), 61–65, for a discussion of the formal, nonformal, and informal forms of education.

2. Jackson W. Carroll, *As One with Authority: Reflective Leadership in Ministry* (Louisville: Westminster/John Knox, 1991), 119–47.

careful consideration. Background elements are "resources that are somewhat more enduring parts of ourselves and the settings' makeup. They are also more tacit than explicit. In contrast, foreground elements are more explicitly brought into play."[3] Background elements include the histories or the complex narratives of persons and their settings. Histories from a Christian viewpoint include the theological perspective, the vision of Christian faith and life that persons and communities maintain. These may be explicit, but more often are implicit. Histories also include the established roles that persons play out in their thought and practice.[4] The foreground elements for Carroll include "scripture and tradition, theories and exemplars from experience (one's own and those of others), elements of the setting or context, and talk back from the situation."[5] The question remains how the leader or teacher can combine or orchestrate these various elements in the process of leading or teaching. Unlike Carroll, I maintain that the Scriptures must maintain primacy among the foreground elements.

Carroll suggests the following dynamic in reflection:

> Throughout the process, the various resources described, background and foreground, will be brought into play. Background resources, which may be more tacit than explicit, are especially important in the way one initially frames issues and one's own role in them. Background resources also often shape which foreground resources are appropriate and how they will be used. Foreground resources help us in understanding the situation's dynamics and the possible responses open to us. This whole reflective conversation implies a kind of systemic thinking as one seeks to construct responses that are both faithful to the church's identity and appropriate to the situation at hand. It is not simply one thing that must be taken into account but a set of interacting factors and resources that must be considered and weighed.[6]

To take into account the various interacting factors, one must have gained expertise, the ability to relate knowledge to concrete

3. Ibid., 160.
4. Ibid., 159–68.
5. Ibid., 168.
6. Ibid., 178.

situations in a systematic way. The stress upon systemic or systematic thinking does not eliminate mystery and intuition, which also must operate in dealing with real situations and persons. Beyond knowledge is the wisdom that persons have acquired through reflection upon experience. Ministry includes both activity and receptivity. Reflection is crucial to foster receptivity to God and God's truth wherever it can be discerned. The exercise of reflection requires of the minister or the teacher the skills of an artist or a craftsperson who listens and responds with care, discernment, and creativity. Reflection in the context of the Christian church requires consideration of theological reflection. Christian teaching assumes fostering participants' theological reflection.

Theological Reflection

Theological reflection is a current area of interest in relation to theological method. The work of Evelyn E. Whitehead and James D. Whitehead has been helpful in this area.[7] The Whiteheads have proposed a model for theological reflection that holds in balance three key sources for understanding the Christian life. Those three sources are tradition, experience, and culture. The source of Christian tradition is multiform in Scripture, theology, and history, and the task in theological reflection is to understand and to interpret this tradition that is a living identity. The source of experience includes both personal and communal experience, and the task in theological reflection is to draw upon the wisdom gained from the practice of life and ministry. Persons need space and luxury to evaluate their and others' experience. The source of culture and society provides a perspective on reality beyond personal and communal experience and tradition. Data from the physical and social sciences and other critical studies provide information that must be incorporated into our understanding of human life. In addition to these three sources or poles, the Whiteheads suggest there are three stages of theological reflection; attending, asserting, and deciding. In attending, persons seek out

7. Evelyn E. Whitehead and James D. Whitehead, *Method in Ministry: Theological Reflection and Christian Ministry* (San Francisco: Harper and Row, 1980).

101

information from the sources of tradition, experience, and culture. In asserting, the information leads people to clarify their views in order to expand and deepen their theological thought. In deciding, persons move to action on the basis of the insights they have gained.[8]

From these three distinct and yet interactive and interdependent sources, Christians in reflection seek to discern points of correlation and convergence, along with points of conflict and divergence. Emphasizing one or two sources to the exclusion of the other(s) creates imbalance and distortion. This does not suggest that the primacy of Scripture is replaced by experience and culture. But it does suggest that insights from Scripture gain greater clarity in conversation with culture and experience. The important insight from the Whiteheads' model is the need to see theological reflection as a dynamic and interactive process that requires careful consideration of a variety of sources. Ronald Gariboldi and Daniel Novotny observe that "it is in the movement from contemplation to action and back again that we discover God."[9] That discovery of God is the goal of theological reflection. The question for Christian teachers is how theological reflection relates to the ministry of Christian education. This question may best be explored in relation to our definition of education.

Excursus: A Definition of Education

Using the Whiteheads' categories, education can be defined as the process of attending to, asserting, and deciding upon content with persons in the context of their community and society. This first suggests that education is a process, an interaction of persons over time. This interaction includes three particular elements: content, persons, and context. Content includes cognitive, affective, intentional, and lifestyle aspects.[10] Persons include teachers,

---

8. Ibid., 21–25.
9. Ronald Gariboldi and Daniel Novotny, in *The Art of Theological Reflection: An Ecumenical Study*, ed. Jean S. Novotny (Lanham, Md.: University Press of America, 1987), 133.
10. James M. Lee discusses the various dimensions of content in *The Content of Religious Instruction: A Social Science Approach* (Birmingham, Ala.: Religious Education Press, 1985).

students or participants, and a host of others represented in the educational encounter. Relationships among persons in education include the immediate participants in a variety of roles. The teacher may also assume the role of an educator-educatee and the student may assume the role of educatee-educator in a relationship of mutuality and dialogue. The context of education is the community and society as well as a variety of educational structures that themselves interact in a configuration or an ecology of education.[11]

The key words in the proposed definition are attending, asserting, and deciding. Attending is the first focus in education, but not to the exclusion of asserting and deciding. Attending can be active in teaching as the teacher shares information and poses problems and questions. Attending can be active in learning as students explore, grapple with, and make connections with the content shared. But attending can also be receptive as both teachers and students engage in listening in depth for meaning. For dialogue to occur, active and receptive listening are required.

Attending relates directly to both critical and reflective thinking in teaching. Critical thinking requires active engagement with thought, reflection, and reason. In addition, receptivity is required to critical questions, underlying issues, and voices forgotten or never heard. Creative thinking encourages active engagement with imagination, playful exploration, and wonder. Creativity implies openness, playfulness, and a willingness to risk. Both critical and creative thinking nurture the hearing of what is not said, the seeing of what is not disclosed. Both give reverence to the necessary space for mystery, awe, and surprise. Both honor the place of excluded knowledge that must be recovered to make us whole.

Asserting, the second focus in education, moves teachers and students to make contrasts and comparisons so as to affirm emerging truth. Asserting brings to some conclusion the process of inquiry. Persons are called upon to own some principles, norms, and/or guidelines that emerge from study. Analysis leads

11. Lawrence A. Cremin describes these educational structures in *Public Education* (New York: Basic, 1976) and *Traditions of American Education* (New York: Basic, 1977).

to possible synthesis or to identifying crucial questions that will require a decision or an action. Asserting requires a personal stance in relation to the wider community and the stances of others. Asserting embraces one's identity while maintaining openness to the contributions of others. Critical and creative thought can eventually lead to positive affirmation as a result of exploring the alternatives and options.

Deciding, the third focus, brings thought processes to the point of action or incarnation. Verbal and intellectual inquiry becomes embodied in commitments to act and launch out. The movement from decision to action must be complemented by the ongoing need for reflection and evaluation. So the process continues with the dynamic interaction of content or tradition, persons or experience, and context or culture. In the process of teaching, reflection provides a key element.

Reflection in Teaching

What Carroll proposes in terms of ministry settings has a direct parallel with what educators propose in relation to the explicit, implicit, and null curricula in teaching. One possible exception is the interaction that Carroll proposes between the background and foreground elements. This interaction requires a holistic vision that educators have not always modeled; rather, they sometimes follow trends without adequately critiquing them. But Elliot W. Eisner is one who has sought to identify a broader vision for the practice of education.

Eisner makes a helpful distinction between the explicit and the implicit curricula in teaching. The explicit curriculum consists of the stated and planned events that are intended to yield certain educational consequences. The explicit curriculum parallels the foreground elements. By contrast, the implicit or hidden curriculum includes the sociological, psychological, and historical dimensions of education, which are usually caught rather than intentionally taught. The implicit curriculum parallels the background elements that Carroll identifies as tacit and implicit in situations. The null curriculum is what is not taught and affects the kinds of options one is able to consider, the alternatives that one can examine, and the perspectives from which one can view a situation or problem.[12]

Naming the null curriculum in teaching incorporates the element of play required to adequately reflect and provide perspective. The interaction of these three curricula is crucial in conceiving of and practicing teaching. Teaching operates at the point of connection between background and foreground elements in educational ministry settings. Teachers must discern the play of these elements in relation to the content and the experiences shared with students.[13] This requires teachers to reflect while they plan to teach, while they teach, and while they evaluate after they have taught. Carroll describes this effort as "reflecting-in-action."[14] Reflecting while teaching can be identified as a metaskill. This metaskill is a capacity for self-analysis and self-evaluation.[15] But it extends beyond the focus upon self to include the contours of the situation and the actions of all participants in the teaching setting.

One can define education as a process of sharing content with persons in the context of their community and society. Reflection is therefore required in relation to the three essential elements of content or curriculum, the persons of the teacher(s) and all participants, and the context of the immediate community along with the wider society. The dynamic and ever-changing interaction of these three elements calls for careful and critical attention from teachers. To effectively do this teachers need a good theory to guide their efforts. A good theory provides insights and access to the process of teaching itself and criteria to use in evaluating teaching from a reflective stance. All teachers have theories that either operate implicitly in their thought and practice or through reflection are explicitly stated and explored in relation to the public. In this work I advocate the need for teachers to make their operating theories explicit through reflection and dialogue with

12. Elliot W. Eisner, *The Educational Imagination: On Design and Evaluation of School Programs*, 2d ed. (New York: Macmillan, 1985), 87–107.

13. For a discussion of the three curricula in educational content, see Pazmiño, *Principles and Practices*, chap. 4, "Educational Content," 91–115.

14. Carroll, *As One with Authority*, 178.

15. See Pazmiño, *Principles and Practices*, 156, for additional insights regarding the concept of a metaskill.

others.[16] The challenge for teachers is to develop through reflection a unifying vision to guide their efforts and to serve as a structure for planning, practice, and evaluation. This vision and structure must be built upon the foundation of authority (chap. 1–3). It is itself authoritative to the extent that the structure is faithful to and consistent with the substructure or foundation. Reflection and dialogue are required to determine whether faithfulness and consistency exist and whether the structure or form can in fact be authoritative. Reflection and reason guide the search for a normative core that undergirds authoritative teaching.

The Place of Reason

Gabriel Fackre describes the place of reason in his discussion of authority in traditional perspectives:

> The place of reason appears in the insistence on the role of philosophy in the theological enterprise (as junior partner), or more recently the facilitating of theology by sociological, psychological, aesthetic, and political insights, and the appeal to standards of logic and evidence. This recourse to natural reason or general experience should be distinguished from the legitimation of reason and experience by its baptism in the waters of faith, as in the reason entailed in "faith seeking understanding" or "experience" as the avenue of confirmation used by the Spirit or in the special grace of conversion. . . . In the case of "reason," however, the role of wider data and reflection, including philosophy, is acknowledged and brought into conversation with Scripture and tradition, albeit always accountable to the scriptural source.[17]

16. See my earlier works, *Foundational Issues* and *Principles and Practices*, to explore some of the dimensions of educational theory that require a consideration of foundations, principles, and guidelines for practice. In addition see Mary C. Boys, *Educating in Faith: Maps and Visions* (San Francisco: Harper and Row, 1989); Ronald Habermas and Klaus Issler, *Teaching for Reconciliation: Foundations and Practices of Christian Education Ministry* (Grand Rapids: Baker, 1992); Michael L. Peterson, *Philosophy of Education: Issues and Options* (Downers Grove, Ill.: InterVarsity, 1986); Jack L. Seymour and Donald E. Miller, eds., *Theological Approaches to Christian Education* (Nashville: Abingdon, 1990); and Jim Wilhoit, *Christian Education and the Search for Meaning*, 2d ed. (Grand Rapids: Baker, 1991).

17. Gabriel Fackre, *The Christian Story: A Pastoral Systematics*, vol. 2, *Authority: Scripture in the Church for the World* (Grand Rapids: Eerdmans, 1987), 96.

Fackre describes reason as having a variety of connotations including "the exercise of the laws of logic, cerebral processes applied to ultimate matters, thematization of intuitive encounters with reality, rigorous empirical investigation, the subjection of all private claims of truth to standards of public inquiry."[18] He also describes various views of thinking that include philosophical, sociopolitical, cultural, and logic-and-evidence views. Each of these views affects the processes of reasoning called upon to verify or warrant one's truth claims.[19]

Theological warrant for the gift and use of reason as a tool for scrutiny comes through recognizing that

> as Christ the eternal Logos of God is the source of both the light in Scripture and the light in creation, their relationship is not out of order. As Christ is our Judge as well as our Advocate, the critical function is also fitting. This is especially true because of our capacity for self-deception is infinite. We need all the help we can get for self-criticism.[20]

Although reason is affirmed, a warning must also be reiterated. Fackre observes that "the Word of Scripture tells us things the wisdom of the world cannot know. In this realm "reason [is] within the bounds of religion."[21]

Truth, Christ, and Scripture

Christians maintain that all truth is God's truth, but that not all truth is of the same order or on the same level. The question

18. Ibid., 137.
19. Ibid., 137–44.
20. Ibid., 175.
21. Ibid., 176. Fackre cites the work of Nicholas P. Wolterstorff, *Reason Within the Bounds of Religion* (Grand Rapids: Eerdmans, 1984). Fackre notes that "Wolterstorff argues that the Christian scholar must be conscious of and employ 'control beliefs' in the conversation with the academy" (176). The control beliefs that Wolterstorff identifies are the fundamental beliefs about the God-creation distinction and relationship that are a result of Christian commitment. These are not exclusively derived from the Scripture and include such beliefs as the Trinity. But they also include the beliefs of creation, sin, salvation, and consummation that are foundational to Christian faith. For discussion of these beliefs see Pazmiño, *Foundational Issues*, 49–63, and *Principles and Practices*, 13–36.

of priority is important and Christians can assert that only the truth revealed in Christ and in Scripture constitutes the ultimate and unifying perspective for learning and life. Anything less can make persons the measure of all things.[22] Faith in Christ and reliance upon Scripture are to have a higher priority over those insights gained through reason. Augustine maintained that if one did not believe in God that person would not come to know the essential truth. In the eleventh century, Anselm of Canterbury stated, "Believe that you may know." Christians suggest that this principle extends beyond religious faith to other endeavors in that believing, as commitment, leads to the knowledge of truth.[23] This stance in Christian teaching implies the need to emphasize personal belief in Christ as the essential foundation for inquiry.

Conscious reliance upon Christ and Scripture follows from the recognition of the presence of sin and the fallen nature of persons, which affects the use of unaided reason not subject to divine revelation. The use of reason is marred or dimmed by sin, but not totally destroyed. Given the presence of personal and corporate sin, Christian teaching must address the areas of moral and ethical character formation to supplement intellectual training, but not in a way that violates the worth and dignity of persons as God's creatures. How the balance is achieved presents a continual challenge in the practice of teaching. For example, what is the place of doubt and questioning that arise from the use of reason? The use of reason implies posing questions and having doubts, even about certain truths that Christians have historically defended. Posing questions becomes the occasion for discovery and inquiry using the capacities of human reason created by God. As noted, Wolterstorff recommends the place of control beliefs. I would suggest the affirmation of foundational beliefs that relate to the interest of love rather than control. This interest in love, in relation to reason and knowledge, is discussed in drawing upon the insights of Parker Palmer. Reason within the suggested bounds makes a significant contribution to the task of sharing the Christian faith.

22. Frank E. Gaebelein, *The Christian, the Arts, and the Truth: Regaining the Vision of Greatness*, ed. Bruce Lockerbie (Portland, Ore.: Multnomah, 1985), 252.
23. Ibid., 86.

Reason operates to insure that the Christian faith is a viable intellectual option. If the challenge of reason is not addressed, Christian faith is reduced to fantasy and ideology. The place of reason and thought is affirmed in Paul's exhortation to the church at Philippi and is worth repeating:

> Finally, beloved, whatever is true, whatever is honorable, whatever is just, whatever is pure, whatever is pleasing, whatever is commendable, if there is any excellence and if there is anything worthy of praise, think about these things. Keep on doing things that you have learned and received and heard and seen in me, and the God of peace will be with you. [Phil. 4:8–9]

The need is to think deeply and seriously about the nature and the purpose of Christian education in terms of its being education. That major focus is an intellectual process that engages persons with transformative Christian content. That content is God's revelation, the gospel that calls for an intellectual, emotional, and active response. Content relates intimately to the persons who participate and the context for teaching. The context is the community of faith, the church, that requires of teachers that we reason together. Reasoning together requires partnership (chap. 2) that includes God and Christian believers past, present, and future. As will be suggested in chapter 6, that partnership can include those not identified as Christian believers, but as seekers and disclosers of truth. For this wider partnership Christian teachers must maintain a perspective that is suggested by Paul's naming of "whatever." This wider perspective affirms the wisdom that all truth is God's truth because of the reality of general revelation and God's common grace. Intellectual diligence is required if Christians are to discern truth or, as the Christian teacher Augustine said, to "spoil the Egyptians."[24]

Spoiling the Egyptians

Augustine's view of "spoiling the Egyptians" draws upon the experience of the nation of Israel when God delivered them from

---

24. This phrase does not demean the wisdom and value of the Egyptian culture. It connotes appropriating insights that are congruent with a Christian world and life view (see also p. 112).

their slavery in Egypt (see Exod. 12:33–36). As the Israelites used the Egyptians' vessels and ornaments of gold and silver to adorn the tabernacle in the wilderness, so Christians can use the wisdom gained from various academic studies and disciplines to enrich and embellish their thought and practice to the end that God might be glorified. The potential difficulty in this spoiling is represented by the construction of the golden calf—an idolatry that displaced theism. The criterion for constructive and faithful use of the spoils was a commitment centered in the worship of and obedience to God. For Christians this requires the use of spoils in ways that are consistent with a Christian world and life view. Consistency requires the use of reason together with other Christians who wrestle with God's revelation. The principle that emerges is that the truth discovered must be consistent with revealed truth. Otherwise reason and reflection deteriorate into worship of the creature instead of the Creator. The operation of reason must be related to the search for truth (chap. 6). Reason is also related to the dominant canons of knowledge that operate historically. This requires of Christian teachers critical awareness of the historical, societal, and cultural context for their reasoning.

Our Context for Reasoning

Reasoning about the Christian faith takes into consideration the heritage of the Enlightenment and developments in postmodernity. Christian teachers must recognize the place of intellectual questioning and doubt in relation to Christian revelation and faith. They must also be aware of the rise of secular faiths—in particular, scientism—as dominant influences in the twentieth century. How does advocacy of a theological foundation for reasoning stand in relation to modern academic disciplines and the search for knowledge? How do theological truths relate to truths discerned through the social sciences and philosophy that have been historical sources for educational thought and practice?[25]

Parker Palmer, in his search for a spirituality of education, proposes that knowledge as understood in our societal context must

25. See Pazmiño, *Foundational Issues*, for my analysis of these foundational questions.

be related to human interests and passions that are often ignored. In his analysis, Palmer proposes that knowledge can be connected with three human interests or passions. These three interests or passions are control, curiosity, and compassion. Knowledge obtained through applied empirical and analytical study generally seeks to gain control over a body of information. Knowledge gained through speculative, historical, and hermeneutical study generally seeks to discover knowledge as an end in itself to satisfy curiosity. The knowledge that liberates is one that Palmer finds described in 1 Corinthians 8:1–3: "Now concerning food sacrificed to idols: we know that 'all of us possess knowledge.' Knowledge puffs up, but love builds up. Anyone who claims to know something does not yet have the necessary knowledge; but anyone who loves God is known by him." This third type of knowledge is associated with compassion or love.[26] This linking of knowledge and love is one expression of orthopathos, which needs to be in relation to orthodoxy and praxis or orthopraxis.[27] Palmer suggests linking knowledge with love, the highest of Christian virtues. But other Christian virtues must also be named in relating education to the formation of character. Doug Sholl has identified a sevenfold pattern of Christian relational content to expand upon the linkage with love in Palmer or the linkage with justice that typifies the work of Lawrence Kohlberg in the area of moral education. Sholl suggests the following pattern: love and justice, truth and faithfulness, forbearance and patience, forgiveness and repentance, edification and encouragement, humility and submission, and prayer and praise.[28]

The current context for reasoning and the acquisition of knowledge values the interests of control and curiosity, to the relative exclusion of love and the other virtues Sholl identified. With the historical rise of scientism this is more apparent. Scientism, as

26. Parker J. Palmer, *To Know As We Are Known: A Spirituality of Education* (San Francisco: Harper and Row, 1983), 6–10.

27. See the discussion in chapter 4.

28. Doug Sholl, "Unity and Uniqueness: A Theology of Christian Relationships," in *Moral Development Foundations: Judeo-Christian Alternatives to Piaget/Kohlberg*, ed. Donald Joy (Nashville: Abingdon, 1983), 188. In addition, see Craig Dykstra, *Vision and Character: A Christian Educator's Alternative to Kohlberg* (New York: Paulist, 1981), 10, for a discussion of virtues.

contrasted with science, denies that truth can be discerned authoritatively through the revelation of the Christian faith and presupposes that empirically based reason is the only medium for gaining knowledge. Huston Smith has pointed out the dangers of the limited reasoning of scientism. Science values control, prediction, objectivity, numbers or quantities, and signs. In contrast, faith values surrender, surprise, subjectivity and objectivity, words, and symbols. Whereas science deals with the instrumental values of utility, usefulness, service, and control, faith deals with the intrinsic values of wonder, awe, reverence, creativity, imagination, and promise. Whereas becoming is the dominant focus of science, being/becoming is the focus of faith.[29] The reasoning advocated in this work does not exclude science and its values, but seeks to include a faith perspective that strives for complementarity and correlation. This approach supports the position of Augustine. Christians can learn from diverse cultures and can be open to receive their contributions while critiquing them from the perspective of a Christian world and life view. This can be called "filtered learning," learning that is filtered through the screen of God's revelation and truth. If persons are to learn from others in formal, nonformal, and informal educational events they need to think. A current interest in the field of education and increasingly in Christian education is teaching for thinking or critical thinking.

Teaching and Critical Thinking

The application of reflection and reason to teaching requires discernment regarding thought processes. Jesus in his teaching ministry encouraged persons to think. His own disciples were asked to think deeply about his difficult teaching (John 6:60–69). Jesus stimulated serious thought and questioning and expected his hearers to carefully consider their personal commitment to the truths he shared. In response to many inquiries, he did not supply simple, ready-made answers to every problem of life. He posed challenges and questions for both Nicodemus (John 3) and the Samaritan woman at the well (John 4). His frequent use of para-

29. Huston Smith, "Excluded Knowledge: A Critique of the Modern Mind Set," *Teachers College Record* (February 1979): 419–45.

bles required his hearers to use various levels of thought to gain understanding. The parabolic forms of his teaching revealed the paradoxes of life and the need for discernment. Jesus expected his students to search their minds and hearts in relation to his teachings and to consider the realities of life.

Christian teachers need to be aware of the tendency to provide simple, ready-made answers for students who need to think for themselves. Teachers need to pose questions that require students to think about issues and real-life problems. Persons need to be encouraged to discover truths through diligence in their study and reflection. Teachers can encourage creative thought as persons make use of their curiosity in exploring various areas of study and in making connections not previously made. This approach requires persons to actively engage in their own education. Such a heightened level of thoughtful activity increases the possibility that persons will appropriate the truths they have discerned or discovered and transfer their learning to new situations.

In relation to thinking, Benjamin Bloom and others identified a taxonomy for the cognitive or thinking dimension of education. Six major categories (in order of complexity) were identified: knowledge or awareness, comprehension, application or transfer of learning, analysis or problem solving, synthesis or creating, and evaluation.[30] Karen A. Wrobbel describes these six stages in relation to Christian education and provides illustrations from her practice:

> The first area is knowledge. The student should be able to recall facts and repeat information. This is basically rote memory that really requires no integration. Reciting the names of the 12 disciples or a memory passage are examples of basic knowledge.
>
> The second level is comprehension. Beyond repetition of facts, the student will understand facts and be able to restate the facts in his/her own words. When a student can not only recite the 10 Commandments in the teacher's words but also restate the Commandments, the student shows comprehension.

30. Benjamin S. Bloom, ed., *Taxonomy of Educational Objectives, Handbook I: Cognitive Domain* (New York: David McKay, 1956); also see the discussion in Habermas and Issler, *Teaching for Reconciliation*, 104–6. For a discussion of the taxonomy see Nicholas P. Wolterstorff, *Educating for Responsible Action* (Grand Rapids: Eerdmans, 1980), 135–48.

Bloom's third level is application. The student applies the comprehended facts to solve problems. The 10 Commandments come alive when the student realizes that pocketing money from mom's purse or wanting to keep up with the Jones' latest acquisition are what the commands are about. Most Christian educators try to include this step but often it's a hurried teacher-prepared application that's tacked on as the closing bell rings.

Level four, which is really the beginning of reflective thinking, is analysis. The student should classify and break down information and discover assumptions. I recently taught apologetics to 11th-and 12th-graders. We used two authors with differing approaches to apologetics, but I didn't do the analysis for the students. As the students analyzed the writings, they discovered that the two authors, although both evangelical, had different theological assumptions. The students ended up discussing Reformed theology, assumptions in Calvinistic and Arminian approaches to election, and a host of other subjects because they analyzed the authors' assumptions for themselves and realized that those assumptions weren't always the same as their own.

Synthesis is the fifth level. The student needs to bring together ideas and compare and contrast their ideas with others'. With the apologetics class, after reading the chapters on the existence of God from both works, I'd ask, "How would Little defend this point? How would Pratt defend this point? How do their approaches differ? Why are they different? Do you agree with either? Why?"

Finally, evaluation is the process of taking ideas and relating them to a standard of judgment and values. The final course assignment for the apologetics students was to write a personal apologetic. Students were encouraged to evaluate the authors and develop their personal apologetic based on their understanding of the Scripture.

Objectives on all six levels will not be developmentally appropriate for younger students, but older students should be regularly challenged by questions requiring analysis, synthesis, and evaluation.[31]

The challenge for Christian teachers is to move students to the higher levels of thinking through posing questions and problems.

31. Karen A. Wrobbel, "Teaching for Thinking: A Must for Christian Education," *Christian Education Journal* 12 (Spring 1992): 149–50.

The challenge is illustrated in the well-known story of one Sunday school teacher who described to her students a small animal with grey fur and a bushy tail who loved to eat nuts. When the children were asked to identify the animal, one boy volunteered his thoughts: "I know the answer is Jesus, but it sure sounds like a squirrel to me." The level of discourse in many Sunday- or church-school contexts encourages the standard response of "Jesus" to many questions that are asked. It is wonderful to name the person of Jesus, but that Jesus would have his disciples think and learn to think as a result of their participation in Christian education.

The practical question remains as to how teachers might encourage learners to use higher levels of thinking. S. Wasserman provides the following suggestions for teacher responses:

1. clarifies an idea ("Is this what you mean?")
2. asks for students' opinions
3. asks for more data ("Tell me more about it.")
4. invites other responses ("Does anyone have other ideas to share?")
5. asks for analysis of idea ("How does this compare with _____?")
6. asks students to extend his/her ideas by asking for a hypothesis or an interpretation
7. raises a new idea that doesn't build on previous ideas ("We have talked about why Christ's ascension was important. What are some of your ideas about the attitudes of the disciples towards the ascension and its effect on them?")
8. accepts student ideas ("I see.")[32]

Teachers can actively foster thinking while they affirm the authority of critical thought, reflection, and reason. The end of such thinking must always be kept in mind. That end is to discern the truth (chap. 6). But while they explore the question of truth, Christian teachers must be aware of various forms of reasoning that characterize the contemporary secular world. These forms

---

32. Ibid., 151, as derived from S. Wasserman, *Put Some Thinking in Your Classroom* (Chicago: Benefic, 1978), 83–96.

actually represent secular faiths that call for the loyalty and commitment of persons to the underlying assumptions and principles. From a theistic perspective each of these secular faiths can be judged as reductionistic, but each serves to identify a level of being that must be considered in theological reflection.

The Challenge of Secular Faiths

The work of Philip H. Phenix is insightful in identifying the various levels of being that are the focus of commitment in secular faiths as compared with the Christian faith. The levels can be arranged in a progression from the simplest level to higher and more complex levels. The levels include matter, life, persons, society, and God.[33] In relation to each of these levels we can name a faith stance that is associated with a particular scientific or philosophical perspective. Each perspective represents a distinct way of viewing the world and a distinct way of reasoning and reflection.

At the lowest level is a faith that focuses on physical concerns, a physical faith. This perspective is present in dialectical or other forms of materialism. For example, strict Marxist and capitalist perspectives focus on economic forces and the ownership of capital. The use of power and forces, as in the study of basic physics, preoccupy advocates of this perspective. Realism is chosen over supernaturalism and salvation is conceived in terms of a new or more efficient economic and sociopolitical order that may require a revolution to establish. The Christian faith affirms the place of the material world as God's creation and the importance of material realities. But life does not consist in the abundance of possessions, and Jesus refused the temptation to change rocks into bread (Matt. 4:1–4; Luke 4:1–4).

The next level has a central concern with life. This biological faith trusts in the evolutionary process and eventual progress. This is the faith of scientific naturalism or humanism. Such a faith relates well with contemporary ecological concerns and a desire to enhance life on a global scale. In this faith perspective

---

33. Philip H. Phenix, lecture presented at Teachers College, Columbia University, New York, New York, 12 December 1979. Phenix's work is drawn and elaborated upon in what follows in discussing secular faiths.

salvation is achieved through education or intellectual enlightenment as better understanding of life and its interdependencies leads to progress. The Christian faith affirms the gift of life and encourages the stewardship of all of creation. But progress and evolution are not inevitable in human history—the realities of corporate and personal sin provide contrary evidence. The challenge is to make history in ways that fulfill Christian values and to confront the real forces of death that are as much present in the world as the forces of life.

The third level of being is that of persons. A faith associated with a focus on persons might be termed a psychological faith associated with personalism or existentialism. From this perspective salvation is achieved through personal enlightenment that celebrates personhood and individuality. A high value is placed on autonomy and the personal quest for meaning. The Christian faith affirms the reality of persons, for God created persons and became a person in Jesus of Nazareth. The value of persons is seen in relation not to autonomy, but to theonomy (see chapter 2 in relation to the models of authority and leadership in the faith community). In fact, the inordinate stress upon individualism and personalism has led to a loss of community and commonweal that many have sought to recover.

The next highest level of being is that of society; a sociological or social-science faith typifies this perspective. Salvation is achieved through critical analysis along with therapy or intervention that either restores a balance or institutes a new order for functioning. The Christian faith affirms understanding the social and corporate character of life, but advocates a more radical transformation of society and community than that proposed in this perspective. Analysis and intervention may not address the underlying problems of human society or acknowledge our interdependence with God to realize solutions.

The highest level of being from a theistic perspective is God, the supernatural being. From the perspective of Christian faith, salvation is achieved as persons receive the gracious gift of God in Christ. The transformation of persons, cultures, societies, and structures is possible through the work of God in partnership with humanity. This transformation affects all the other levels of being. Integration is possible as persons, communities, and societies are centered upon God not only in their reflection, but also in their life together. Theological reflection is central to affirming a theistic perspective and to exploring the question of truth in an age of religious and cultural plurality.

Conclusion

Reason must operate within the bounds and bonds of faith in Christian teaching. The bounds or boundaries are secured through theological authority and the institutional authority that holds one's reasoning up to scrutiny of dialogue and discourse in the faith community and various publics (including academic disciplines). Teachers are called to love God with their minds and to actively engage the rigorous discipline of study. While they engage in this study teachers must also love God with their hearts, souls, and strength, and in doing so share life as well as doctrine with students. The fruits of intellectual inquiry must always be held both firmly and in an open-handed manner. The open-handed manner enables others to carefully examine what is offered by the teacher and to make contributions. Such is the privilege and responsibility of reasoned and reasonable teaching in the Christian tradition. The search for truth by Christian teachers calls for their best efforts in using the gift of reason.

6

Authority of Truth in an Age of Pluralism

At the trial of Jesus as recorded in the Gospel of John, Pilate asks Jesus, "What is truth?" (18:38). Pilate was responding to Jesus' statements: "You say that I am a king. For this I was born, and for this I came into the world, to testify to the truth. Everyone who belongs to the truth listens to my voice" (John 18:37). Denise Lardner Carmody contends that "the passionate commitment of the teacher to the elusive truth being pursued is the crux of educational authority."[1]

1. Denise Lardner Carmody, "Authority and Responsibility in the Class-room," *The Council of Societies for the Study of Religion Bulletin* 19 (February 1990): 3.

The pursuit of truth undergirds all education worthy of the efforts of both teachers and students. But Carmody's characterization of truth as "elusive" can be both affirmed and critiqued from the perspective of the Christian faith and the claims attributed to Jesus Christ. The truth is elusive in the sense that no one person or group can claim to possess the truth in its ultimate and final form, except for Jesus the Christ. The human capacity for truth is circumscribed by the limitations of both experience in general and reason in particular (chaps. 4 and 5 respectively). The truth must also be seen as requiring a holistic head, heart, and hand response of persons to what is discovered or disclosed. This response requires a lifelong pursuit. But the truth is not elusive in the sense of the Christian claim that truth is revealed in the person of Jesus Christ. The writer of the gospel of John claims this: "The law indeed was given through Moses; grace and truth came through Jesus Christ" (John 1:17). Truth is embodied, incarnated, in Jesus of Nazareth; it is not elusive to those who seek to be his disciples: "Then Jesus said to the Jews who had believed in him, 'If you continue in my word, you are truly my disciples; and you will know the truth, and the truth will make you free'"(John 8:31–32).

The call that comes to the Christian teacher requires a passionate love for truth. This can be proposed as one element of the orthopassion or orthopathos that Samuel Solivan has named.[2] The embrace of truth includes not only the response of the reasoning mind, but also the joy and delight of the loving heart. Both mind and heart are engaged as persons seek to live out the truth.

To love and to pursue the truth requires sensitivity to the context in which that love and search is undertaken. The context sets the parameters for the active search for truth without eliminating the ultimate source for truth. The ultimate source for truth, from the perspective of the Christian faith, is embodied in the person of Jesus Christ who claimed to be the truth. Those who seek to be disciples of Jesus are promised access to the truth. Access to truth occurs in particular historical contexts that require our evaluation.

2. Samuel Solivan, "Orthopathos: Interlocutor between Orthodoxy and Praxis," *Andover Newton Review* 1 (Winter 1990): 19–25.

Our Context for the Search of Truth

Truth can be found in many places. Christian truth and its implicit authority is exercised in a marketplace of diverse truth claims that are supported by religious and secular faiths. From the perspective of the Christian faith, the essential source of both truth and authority is Jesus Christ. Christians affirm the Christ revealed in Scripture and witnessed to by the church through the ages. But if Christ is also affirmed as the *logos*, the Word (John 1), the image of the invisible God revealed throughout creation (Col. 1), the reflection of God's glory (Heb. 1), and the first and last living one (Rev. 1), then Christians can discern truths in a wide variety of sources that are consistent with God's special revelation in Jesus of Nazareth. *As Christians we can learn much from others who are not like us.* To refuse to learn from others can represent a stance of arrogance.

In 1974, at its meeting in Accra, Ghana, the Faith and Order Commission of the World Council of Churches engaged in a study on the theme "How Does the Church Teach Authoritatively Today?"[3] Four study groups explored the question and gathered in a consultation in Odessa, then the Soviet Union, that issued a report. The report identified four aspects of the contemporary context requiring attention if Christians are to teach authoritatively. Those four aspects are change, pluralism, participation, and reception.[4] In relation to each of these aspects it is possible to explore the authority of truth that is sought in Christian teaching.

Change

In chapter 1 the proposed definition of authority named the matter of foundations that are unchanged and unchanging to ground one's perspective. If truth is in fact truth, then the as-

---

3. The use of World Council of Churches documents is intended to provide a challenge for my evangelical readers and to support the active role of evangelicals in wider ecumenical discussions with something valuable to contribute and to gain from dialogue. My stance as an ecumenical evangelical Christian supports this use.

4. Faith and Order Commission, "How Does the Church Teach Authoritatively Today?: Faith and Order Paper No. 91," *The Ecumenical Review* 31 (January 1979): 77–93.

sumption is that it is also unchanged and unchanging. How then is it possible to accommodate change in the search for foundations that are sure and unchanging? How is it possible to affirm both continuity and change in exploring an authoritative base for teaching?

The World Council study identified the need to adapt teaching to the needs of the present time. It viewed change not as random innovation and betrayal of the gospel, but as a faithful witness to the past that itself incorporates reformation and transformation. It advocated that teaching take place in constant interaction with the world.[5] Authoritative teaching must be sensitive to the context of the community, society, and world in which it takes place. But the focus on the world and its changing contours must not override primary concern for the essential content and a corresponding concern for the persons participating. This is suggested by the model of the educational trinity that affirms both the content and the context of teaching along with the persons involved.

In Christian teaching the stress upon contextualization (context) must be complemented by a stress upon textualization (content). Gabriel Fackre recognizes this dynamic: "The truth God discloses in and through Scripture is truth for all that becomes by its Author's intention truth for us in cultural context and truth for me in personal context."[6] Contextualization focuses upon truth for us in the context of the community and/or society with its particular culture or cultures. It can also focus upon truth for me in the realm of personal experience, intuition, introspection, and reflection. But textualization wrestles with truth for all.[7] The modern interest in truth for me and us has too readily jettisoned the search for truth for all. The birthright of the Christian faith is the search for the truth for all along with the truth for us and me. This birthright has been too readily sold for a porridge of relativism and relevance that fails to wrestle with eternal verities and absolutes. A complementary danger is, of course, to avoid contextual-

5. Ibid., 87.
6. Gabriel Fackre, *The Christian Story: A Pastoral Systematics*, vol. 2, *Authority: Scripture in the Church for the World* (Grand Rapids: Eerdmans, 1987), 212.
7. Ibid.

ization while one embraces textualization.[8] Another danger that some Christians have identified is the contemporary reality of pluralism in modern life, particularly religious pluralism.[9]

Pluralism

The World Council study named pluralism as a new appreciation of the variety of perspectives in the Christian faith and in life. It maintained that acceptance of pluralism does not undermine unity. Authoritative teaching seeks to maintain the Christian church in unity while not imposing uniformity. Authoritative teaching does not deny pluralism and creative difference. Unity was seen as possible in relation to eucharistic fellowship and common mission and witness. This concern for pluralism was distinguished from indifferentism and relativism, which refuses to distinguish between truth and error.[10] The additional challenge in relation to pluralism is the encounter among diverse faith communities that can result in interfaith dialogue and cooperation.

In the Bible one finds a number of examples of encounters with other religious perspectives. Paul made use of pagan culture to explore the distinctives of the gospel (Acts 17). In various portions of the Scripture, writers draw upon the Apocrypha in their discussion of religious matters. Jesus himself drew upon the account of the unjust steward, and this fact suggests that his disciples can learn from the people of this age or world (Luke 16). The Scriptures themselves reflect extensive drawing upon Semitic and Greek cultures and traditions as a means by which to disclose the glories of God. This was also my experience in graduate work.

It was my privilege during graduate studies at Columbia University to complete a course that explored education and the faiths of humankind. This course, taught by Professor Philip H. Phenix, included persons from diverse faith expressions; participants were able to read and to hear from advocates from within

8. See Robert W. Pazmiño, *Principles and Practices of Christian Education: An Evangelical Perspective* (Grand Rapids: Baker, 1992), 158–61, for a discussion of the reductionism that plagues educational ministries.
9. This chapter explores an encounter with religious pluralism. A related issue is that of multicultural pluralism; I have addressed it in other writings as noted in the select bibliography. See also additional sources listed there.
10. "How Does the Church Teach Authoritatively?" 87.

each faith community. The faith communities we explored included both historical religious faiths and the secular faiths of the modern world. The historic faiths discussed included Hinduism, Buddhism, Taoism, Judaism, Roman Catholicism, Eastern Orthodoxy, Protestantism, and Islam. The secular faiths explored included communism, scientific humanism, psychologism, existentialism, and personalism. Some of these secular faiths are distinctly atheistic, whereas others allow for theistic insights. Through the exploration of these various faith expressions I was able to gain a greater appreciation of my Christian faith identity while being open to the truths named by other faiths. Fackre describes this dynamic as involving both the scandal of particularity, in relation to Christian distinctives, and the scandal of universality, in relation to the operation of common grace and general revelation within other faiths.[11] The scandal of particularity recognizes the distinctive claims of Jesus as the Christ, the fullest revelation of God and the only begotten Son of God. The scandal of universality recognizes God's intention for all of humanity and creation, since Christ was the Lamb slain before the foundation of the world. It also recognizes God's sovereignty and mission before and beyond the Christian church. In relation to each of the faiths explored I will mention key insights I gained as a Christian educator, with the hope that others will be encouraged to gain insights from dialogue within a pluralistic religious and faith setting.[12]

Hinduism

Hinduism spoke to me of the inconsistencies of life that can be affirmed through the intuitive encounter of wholeness.[13] Such an

11. Fackre, *Christian Story*, vol. 2, *Authority*, 278. Also see Gabriel J. Fackre, "The Scandals of Particularity and Universality," *Mid-Stream* 12 (January 1983): 32–52.

12. The following analysis of various faith perspectives may err on the side of oversimplification; the discussion is limited to the books selected by Phenix. Nevertheless the discussion serves to illustrate the potential usefulness of wider dialogue and how a constructive exploration of other faith perspectives may occur in a particular course structure. For a more detailed treatment of this theme see Norma H. Thompson, ed., *Religious Pluralism and Religious Education* (Birmingham, Ala: Religious Education Press, 1988).

13. R. C. Zaehner, *Hinduism* (Oxford: Oxford University Press, 1962).

124

encounter views those inconsistencies as an illusion veiling the essential integration of all of life. I refute the Hindu characterization of individuality and historicity as illusion, but affirm the sense of unity that is realized only in the midst of variety. The basic unity of all things cannot deny the rich variety and complexity that also characterizes life. I honor the unique creation and expression of creation that each individual person is. I celebrate the richness and the variety of God's created life and God's reality as encountered uniquely in each person. Hinduism's pluralistic nature and its affirmation of many paths confirms for me the unique path and pilgrimage of faith that each individual may have. As Hinduism is complex, so is the reality of Christian faith in the heart and life of each disciple of Christ.

Hinduism challenged me in its relative freedom from divisive dogmatic assumptions, even in the midst of its complexity. Christian faith, by contrast, has been plagued by division, which dogma has supported. My encounter with Hinduism has helped me to deepen my quest for an ecumenical faith that fulfills Jesus' prayer for unity (John 17). The apostle Paul encouraged the Christians in Ephesus to make every effort to "maintain the unity of the Spirit in the bond of peace" (Eph. 4:3).

Buddhism

Christmas Humphreys claimed that "Buddhism, like any other form of relative truth, must vary with the individual, and grow for him with his individual growth."[14] This perspective directly challenged me to consider to what extent the absolute and exclusive claims of Christian faith could be relativized to allow for individual and contextual differences. Here is the question of the relationship between contextualization and textualization posed by Fackre. Contextualization cannot distort the essentials revealed in the text or the content of the Christian faith. But historical developments in religious faiths indicate movement to a more universal expression in the sense of embracing the universal character of the faith that transcends particular historical expressions.

Buddhism's Middle Way between asceticism and self-indulgence confirmed my concern in faith to maintain a balance be-

---

14. Christmas Humphreys, *Buddhism* (New York: Penguin, 1976), 15.

tween intellect and emotion, between form and freedom, and between a conservative and a radical position in life. My concern for balance involves the need to give attention to both dimensions of life by realizing a middle way between extreme orientations. Too often, much is forgotten in popular movements in faith expressions. The Middle Way can offer a comprehensive perspective that helps us to see the truth holistically and to recognize the place of paradox in faith and life.

Taoism

Taoism represents a faith that is able to integrate and accommodate very diverse perspectives and ideas. Taoism honors the place of paradox in life and faith. The Christian faith strives to realize a holistic and comprehensive world view, but Christians sometimes ignore the place of paradox. In an age of pluralism I am confronted with the exclusive nature of some of my theological conceptions. What I so readily forget or disregard may be important to consider.

Taoism respects the place of rational knowledge, intuitive knowledge, and no-knowledge, whereas I too often operate only in the rational area and fail to appreciate the manifold ways of knowing. "No-knowledge" is the recognition of the place of mystery and the extrarational elements of life that a supernatural faith affirms. Taoism reveals the nervous haste and activity of Western society that fails to recognize realities beyond the search for rational knowledge and the control of resources. The advance of society through the sciences has too often forgotten that which is transparent or ultimate in human experience. Taoism names the complexities of knowledge that education must consider. This consideration encourages a stance of openness and tolerance. R. G. H. Siu in *The Tao of Science* defines wisdom as the "the artful way in which rational knowledge, intuitive knowledge, and no-knowledge are mastered, handled, integrated, and applied."[15] This conception of wisdom necessitates practical application or incarnation with the ongoing interaction of action and reflection.

15. R. G. H. Siu, *The Tao of Science: An Essay on Western Knowledge and Eastern Wisdom* (Cambridge, Mass.: M.I.T. Press, 1957), 84.

Christian educators are task theologians who seek to foster the handling, integrating, and applying of Christian knowledge to individual and corporate responsibilities. This is referred to as wisdom. But whatever system or model one proposes, one must also recognize its limitations. All of the world cannot be encompassed in any system or model and the blind spots must be named. Taoism thus encourages the place of self-criticism and the need for openness in teaching.

Judaism

Judaism, from the perspective of Abraham Heschel, has much to offer the Christian faith, for the two have a common kinship and heritage. Thus Judaism and Christianity have a relationship distinct in kind from that with other world religions. Heschel reminded me that Jesus was a Jew who deeply embraced the spirit of Judaism.

Heschel also reintroduced me to the essential place of joy and wonder in both life and education. He speaks of the ecstasies of worship that are embodied in everyday life. Judaism affirms the joy that is life and the goodness inherent in the creation that yet veils the mystery of God. Judaism centers upon God's covenant, activity, faithfulness, and interest directed towards persons. Passion and feeling emerge from the prophetic encounter with the living and seeking God. This God relates to persons not only in holiness, but also in love and personal concern. Thus Heschel stated that education should include not only the empowerment of persons, but also the nurturing of a sense of wonder, awe, and joy.[16] This is a perspective I embrace and celebrate for Christian teaching.

Educators must often call into question, or at least into consideration, that which is forgotten in the faddism that characterizes educational programs and theological trends. Heschel speaks about having to love God in order to know God and about how a Jew is asked to take a leap of action, rather than a leap of

16. Abraham J. Heschel, *Between God and Man: An Interpretation of Judaism from the Writings of Abraham Heschel,* ed. Fritz A. Rothschild (New York: Free Press, 1959), 37. Also see Victor Gross, *Educating to Reverence: The Legacy of Abraham Heschel* (Bristol, Ind.: Wyndham Hall, 1989).

thought, in a faith response to God's love. These insights reaffirm the vital relationship between faith and action, an insight that is forgotten in personalized understandings of faith and salvation. Judaism challenges Christian faith in terms of taking seriously the ethical implications of faith. These ethical implications include both personal and social ethics. Heschel pointed out that modern persons often care only for personal needs rather than for being needed.[17] Worshiping at the altar of needs does not satisfy deep human longings. This is a particular challenge to Christian educators who stress an educational model centered on the satisfaction of needs.[18]

Islam

Islam uniquely joins the social and religious spheres, eliminating the Western dichotomy between the religious and the profane, and embraces society as a sphere of the spirit.[19] Islam attempts to realize what liberation movements have sought through transforming society; it provides a structure for society that is clearly delineated and specified. Christianity has struggled with the dialectic between the spiritual and the social, political, and economic spheres of life. Islam resolves this tension, although from my perspective it does so in a rigid and imposed way. My uneasiness with Islam is related to the cost of this integration in terms of human freedom and individuality.

Islam at points appears to be a reaction to a vulgarized form of Christian faith that neglected its prophetic task and social dimension. Islam attempts to deal explicitly, forcefully, and directly with the human dilemma of fragmentation through a completely integrated way of life. It claims to have surpassed and superseded Christianity; and, from the viewpoint of integration into social and political realities, it has. My question is At what cost? The costs may be too high in terms of human freedom and diversity. But Islam challenges the Christian faith in terms of the need for a public theology.

17. Ibid., 129.
18. For additional discussion of this question of needs see Pazmiño, *Principles and Practices*, 33–34, 162.
19. Seyed Hossein Nasr, *Ideals and Realities of Islam* (Boston: Beacon, 1975).

Christian Traditions

Course participants explored the three historical divisions of Roman Catholicism, Orthodoxy, and Protestantism. In relation to the broader Judeo-Christian perspective, Phenix named some distinctives that were insightful. Judaism has tended to stress the codes and practices of faith within the law and its connection with life. This focus upon the moral and ethical dimensions of life results in action and service. Roman Catholicism has tended to stress the institutional and organizational dimensions of faith within various structures and systems. This results in a focus upon the political and broad social dimensions of life. Orthodoxy has tended to stress the rites, rituals, and sacraments of faith embodied in symbols and images. This results in a focus upon the aesthetic and affective dimensions of life that hold a potential for integration. Protestantism has tended to stress the creeds and beliefs of faith embodied in doctrines and theological statements. This results in a focus upon the intellectual and conceptual dimensions of life. Beyond Phenix's analysis it is possible to identify a recent historical expression of the Judeo-Christian tradition in various emerging Pentecostal, charismatic, and renewal movements both within and outside of traditional faith communities. Pentecostalism has tended to stress the spiritual and mystical experiences of faith that restore a sense of joy and fulfillment. This results in a focus upon the relational and communal dimensions of life that include the presence and ministry of the Holy Spirit. These descriptions tend to generalize various traditions, but they also serve to highlight the particular gifts and graces that each tradition can offer to persons and the wider community of faith.

Roman Catholicism

Roman Catholicism, as represented in Jacques Maritain's *Challenges and Renewals*, synthesizes philosophy and faith.[20] Maritain sought a comprehensive understanding of being and life and he evidences a natural spirituality of intelligence. With Maritain I share the concern about the loss of reason and the escape

20. Jacques Maritain, *Challenges and Renewals*, ed. Joseph W. Evans and Leo R. Ward (Cleveland: World, 1966).

from reason that typifies some modern thought. I share this concern because I value rationality within the faith, and I reject the sense of human autonomy that fails to be conscious of God as revealed within history. But distinct from Maritain, I extend the effects of sin to include the rational and spiritual preconscious or unconscious of persons. This sets a definite limit on the use of reason (chap. 5). But Maritain confirmed for me the uniqueness of religion over against philosophy. He viewed religion as involving a relation of person to person with all the risk, mystery, dread, confidence, delight, and torment that lies in such a relationship.[21] This distinction challenged me to maintain a more active interaction between religion and philosophy, between faith and reason. Yet, as a Protestant, I question whether God is rational in terms of human categories and understandings outside of faith. This is where I depart from Maritain's natural theology. Nevertheless, I agree with Maritain that Christianity does not impose a particular political philosophy, but operates to critique all political systems in its call for justice, righteousness, and love in all human structures and relationships.[22]

Orthodoxy

With the works of Nicholas Berdyaev and Fyodor Dostoevsky I entered the faith perspective of Eastern Orthodoxy, which affirms human freedom with its inherent contradictions.[23] I struggle with the exercise of freedom within education, where the teacher with inherent authority and power seeks to empower students so that they can exercise freedom responsibly. The danger is for the teacher, with every good intention, to impose one way of knowing and not allow for the autonomy of students. But autonomy itself cannot be the ultimate goal; a second or greater freedom must be considered. This second freedom is a freedom in the truth, a freedom in Christ that is realized in community with others. This requires a movement from dependence to independence (the first freedom) to interdependence (the second freedom realized fully in Christ).

21. Ibid., 67.
22. Ibid., 306.
23. Nicholas Berdyaev, *Dostoevsky* (New York: New American Library, 1974).

130

My Christian faith is challenged in this perspective because an affirmation of freedom inherently permits the possibility of oppression and injustice. This possibility calls for the exercise of responsible freedom. For example: Christians stand against evil that is present within them; but do they also stand for the right of others to choose the evil? The dilemma posed by Dostoevsky and Berdyaev is one question in the formation of a public theology. For Dostoevsky, Marxist socialism embodied the very principle and spirit of Antichrist in sacrificing human freedom. Marxism called for the apocalyptic realization of salvation from misery and suffering through social, economic, and political liberation. Dostoevsky's description of the legend of the grand inquisitor in *The Brothers Karamazov* points out that Jesus did not succumb to the temptations of Satan in the desert (Luke 4:1–13); so Christians must not succumb to the inadequate solutions offered by socialism to deal with human suffering, which is a result of human freedom. This critique is a sobering corrective to utopian concepts in Christian social action and ministry. Human freedom holds the potential of both good and evil.

Protestantism

Protestantism was explored in the work of H. Richard Niebuhr, *Radical Monotheism and Western Culture*.[24] This work is characteristic of the intellectual focus upon beliefs and creeds in much of Protestantism. Niebuhr affirmed the vital connection between faith and reason in which both permeate and interact with each other. He saw the task of theology as reasoning in faith and criticism of faith. Reasoning in faith was the focus of chapter 5, but the criticism of faith raises the important question of doubt in relation to teaching.

Ronald T. Habermas suggests that three types of doubt can be identified from the Scriptures. These three types of doubt can affect the teaching of the Christian faith and the experience of students. Emotional doubt as experienced by John the Baptist (Matt. 11:1–19) was constructive doubt as John wrestled with the awareness of his imminent death and with the veracity of Jesus'

24. H. Richard Niebuhr, *Radical Monotheism and Western Culture* (New York: Harper, 1960).

claims to be the messiah. The cognitive or factual doubt of Thomas (John 20:19–29) can also be described as constructive as he sought evidence for the claims of Jesus' resurrection. These two examples of constructive doubt led to faith as a result of an open-ended search for the truth. But the volitional doubt of the religious leaders in response to Jesus' claims (Mark 11:27–12:13; Matt. 15:1–20) was destructive as they refused to consider the evidence of Jesus' ministry.[25]

The challenge posed for Christian educators is to maintain creative tension between faith and reason, affirming the place of constructive doubt and avoiding destructive doubt. The destructive tendency that concerns me as a Protestant is reasoning outside of faith and a negation of biblical accounts as providing normative categories for present-day faith experience. Whereas Niebuhr saw faith as both a trust or confidence in a value center and a commitment of fidelity and loyalty, I maintain that the *object* of one's faith is crucial. That object is the living God revealed in Jesus Christ. In terms of the object of faith, Niebuhr views the stance of radical monotheism as having the value center of the principle of being itself. I recognize the power of such an understanding, but question the ultimate impact of Niebuhr's formulations. The Christian faith and the meaning of faith symbols are grounded in historical realities and not just in the principle of being itself. My concern is that Niebuhr may lose this grounding.

Niebuhr, for me, escapes from reason at the point at which he divorces the faith symbol from normal rational categories by means of paradox. Paradox is present in faith and life, but paradox does not negate the meaning of Christian foundations. His assertion that radical monotheism affects political and academic life challenged me. I wonder if these conceptions are capable of being realized except in very individual terms as one influences the social realities and structures of life. But I can see how for Niebuhr all of life is permeated by the fundamental covenant between God and humanity. Every action and relation holds the potential for recognizing and committing oneself to being, better stated "to God." I question whether individuals have the potential to actu-

---

25. Ronald T. Habermas, "Doubt Is Not a Four-Letter Word," *Religious Education* 84 (Summer 1989): 403–4.

alize proper relationships through what amounts to primarily intellectual insights concerning ontology and faith experience. In other words, Niebuhr maintains that a radical monotheist must have certain cognitive and intellectual capabilities to realize a dynamic faith. I question this stance and Niebuhr's relatively exclusive intellectual focus on faith. I also question whether Niebuhr's insights are radical enough for the personal and corporate transformation needed in the world today.

Secular Faiths

In addition to the historic religious faiths, the course with Professor Phenix gave careful consideration to the dominant secular faiths in modern society. Advocates of these faiths hold as much allegiance to them as the advocates of traditional faiths hold to theirs. These faiths also include value and belief commitments that parallel traditional religious beliefs. They address the common dilemmas of human existence with truth stances that strive to be comprehensive. The five secular faiths considered were communism, scientific humanism, psychologism, existentialism, and personalism. These secular faiths represent major challenges to the Christian ministries of evangelism and teaching.

Communism

The faith of communism, though recently discredited in Eastern Europe and the former Soviet Union, still represents one perspective advocated for addressing the needs of developing nations. Communism maintains that the relations of production condition and determine the character of all human institutions, activities, and purposes.[26] The Christian faith also recognizes the essential dimension of the body and activity in the human community. The challenge posed by communism is the need for justice, equity, and liberation in economic, political, and social relationships. For Christians this challenge is to take seriously the ways faith influences economic, social, and political systems and structures. But I do not hold to the priority and the absolutely determinative nature of economic factors in human life. Ideas and

26. Maurice Cornforth, *Communism and Human Values* (New York: International Publishers, 1972).

spiritual realities interact with economic factors and so condition reality. This critique applies to both strict communist and capitalist perspectives on life.

Marxist apocalyptic and millenarian conceptions that revolution will usher in a new age of liberation do not correlate with social realities. Communist solutions to oppression and injustice in economic structures are simplistic; they do not recognize the full extent of the human dilemma that includes the potential for continued oppression under any form of economic structure. A communist society can not recreate or eliminate the inherent weaknesses of human nature while maintaining human freedoms. The Christian faith recognizes the need for social action, but it also recognizes the limited potential for complete justice and liberation outside of divine intervention. The contours of Christ's reign transcends all economic and political positions, and that reign calls into judgment all human structures and systems. Truth is not limited to and determined by the economic and class analysis proposed by communism.

Scientific Humanism

The secular faith of scientific humanism was explored in relation to the work of the progressive educator John Dewey.[27] Dewey called for the liberation of the religious from all that is supernatural and associated with organized religions. His overriding concern was that this association vulgarized and nullified the creative and constructive potential of the religious impulse to realize integration and unification in life. But Dewey became incensed with the letter and the structure of historical religion and ignored its essential spirit, dynamic, and organism that can not be separated from the supernatural.

Dewey identified the religious quality with a commitment to an ideal that transcends human difficulty and adversity. He presents to Christian faith the antisupernatural challenge of enlightened culture. Dewey pointed up the danger of the dualism between the natural and supernatural and the resulting bifurcation of knowledge. His concern that the need for divine depen-

---

27. John Dewey, *A Common Faith* (New Haven: Yale University Press, 1934).

134

dence and support can delimit human thought and inquiry must be heeded. Yet Dewey portrayed an extreme optimism regarding the human potential for affection, compassion, justice, equality, and freedom. He called for the construction of the City of Humankind, an idea that fails to take into account human sin in both its personal and corporate expressions. By comparison, as a Christian I stand in a countercultural position in affirming the supernatural. The supernatural imbues life with transformational and recreative power.

Psychologism

Psychologism was explored in the work of Erich Fromm.[28] Fromm defines religion as any system of thought and action shared by a group that gives a frame of reference or orientation and an object of devotion. He viewed the essential question as whether a religion furthers human development and unfolds human powers or paralyzes them. In North American culture, the Christian faith has been laid over with what Fromm describes as the modern idolatry of power, success, and the authority of the market. Often the dominant "American" (referring to the United States and ignoring the other Americas) church has replaced radical discipleship with an uncritical acceptance of cultural values. Fromm caricatures and criticizes Christian theology, especially in the Reformed tradition, as resulting in self-alienation. But Fromm fails to recognize the affirmation of human power and potential by virtue of creation that endows persons with creative powers. Fromm commends pyschoanalysis that aims primarily at the cure of the soul, at the optimal development of human potentialities and individuality. The Christian faith does affirm this aim and recognizes the intrinsic worth and significance of each person, but as a creature of God and thus worthy of love and concern.

I value Fromm's concern for human integration and wholeness, but this quest must be set within the framework of an encounter and a relationship with God. Psychologism too readily results in a preoccupation with the self at the expense of the wider

28. Erich Fromm, *Psychoanalysis and Religion* (New Haven: Yale University Press, 1950).

135

community and society. The Christian claim is that the ultimate healer of the human soul and reconciler of humanity is God in the person of Jesus Christ.

Existentialism

A fourth secular faith is existentialism, represented in the work of Karl Jaspers and others.[29] Jaspers brought me on a journey dealing with the interiority of life and thought that revealed some of the unspoken dilemmas of faith. He viewed the essence of philosophy as the search for truth, a search that parallels the faith pilgrimage of the thinking Christian. Jaspers spoke of the drives of wonder, doubt, and the sense of forsakenness that along with the absence of communication serve as sources to wisdom. These same sources can serve as prods for one's faith quest. Jaspers described the ultimate situations of death, suffering, chance, and guilt. These situations raise ultimate questions and provide the occasion for the expression of ultimate concern that Paul Tillich described as faith.[30]

Jaspers's way to wisdom deepened my affirmation of the Christian faith as it relates to the dilemmas of human existence and freedom. He speaks of how wonder leads to knowledge, doubt to certainty, forsakenness to the self, and the absence of communication to authentic communication. This may not always be the case because of the presence of sin. The other Christian distinctive, not noted by Jaspers, is that the Christian search for meaning is transcribed within a community of faith that sustains and confronts the individual self. Jaspers's principles of philosophical faith could well be a ground upon which to explore the Christian faith, except for a further assertion he makes: "God does not speak through the commands and the revelations of other men but in man's selfhood and through his freedom, not from without but from within."[31] The Christian faith perspective includes revelation from without; it seeks to affirm revelation from both without and within, and persons can explore the interface between these two dimensions of life. Existential elements

29. Karl Jaspers, *Way to Wisdom: An Introduction to Philosophy* (New Haven: Yale University Press, 1954).
30. Paul Tillich, *Dynamics of Faith* (New York: Harper, 1957).
31. Jaspers, *Way to Wisdom*, 90.

are present in the Christian faith, but there is more beyond the existential experience to be affirmed. Existentialism focuses so much on the individual person that legitimate concerns for the content and the context of truth can be lost.

Personalism

The fifth secular faith considered in this survey was personalism as expressed in the work of Martin Buber.[32] It must be noted that Buber's work cannot be totally characterized as secular in view of his commitment to the revival of Hasidism in Judaism. His work can bridge a discussion of secular and religious faiths and question a division between the sacred and the secular aspects of life. But personalism divorced from religious faith has typified popular culture in the West.

With Buber one sees the need to eventually connect the quest for meaning and life to historic religious faith (in his case, Judaism). Buber approaches faith and truth through personal relationships, and his personalism celebrates God's presence in all of life. Buber's call is to see each person as created in the image of the personal God and therefore worthy of love and understanding. Through personal encounters with others, transformation and the experience of mutual concern are possible. Thus Buber reveals the hub of human experience and a central element of the Christian faith. The challenge for Christians is the actualization of such quality encounters with others and with God. Christians are challenged with how they respect and honor each and every person as a creature of God, whether those persons embrace the Christian faith or not.

Buber views relation as reciprocity; relation calls for mutual dialogue, encounter, and love that enable the other to be. Yet, he observed, both the history of the human race and the history of the individual reveal a "progressive increase of the It-world."[33] Buber saw true community as coming into reality when all participants stand in a living, reciprocal relationship to a single living center and to one another.[34] The struggle for the Christian

32. Martin Buber, *I and Thou*, trans. Walter Kaufman (New York: Charles Scribner's Sons, 1970).
33. Ibid., 87.
34. Ibid., 94.

community is the need to view the full extent of the global community and to have an openness to all persons. The dominant understanding of community within the Christian faith tends to be particularistic, parochial, and exclusive. Buber shatters this particularistic view and expands community to include all persons, regardless of their religious affiliation. The challenge for me is to affirm both the universality of the human community of which Buber speaks and the particularity of the Christian faith community. Both communities are engaged in the search for truth.

Buber stresses the personal dimension of God's being and does so at points to the exclusion of considering divine transcendence. Transcendence is expressed within personal encounter. Similarly, Buber views Jesus as unconditional I-Thou, but not in terms of his uniqueness over against all other persons. In these areas my faith is clarified. My understanding of the Christian affirms the vital personal dimension of human life, but also affirms the distinctive historical formulations concerning the persons of God the Father, Son, and Holy Spirit.

Concluding Insights

My survey of both religious and secular faiths serves to point up the potential of wrestling with truth in a pluralistic context. Such a wrestling can serve to both affirm one's Christian identity with its distinctives and foster an openness to others. Constance J. Tarasar, an Orthodox educator, advocates this approach to religious pluralism. She proposes that we educate for both identity and openness.[35] Truth can be discerned in both the particulars of Christian faith and the insights from other religious perspectives. Reinhold Niebuhr observed that one of the tasks of Christians is to discern "a wise correlation between the truths of faith and all the truths which emerge from the various disciplines of culture."[36] The educator Frank E. Gaebelein maintained that in Christian education, we have the duty to point all persons to the highest examples of excellence, namely, the most excellent of all

35. Constance J. Tarasar, "The Minority Problem: Educating for Identity and Openness," in *Religious Pluralism and Religious Education*, ed. Norma H. Thompson (Birmingham, Ala.: Religious Education Press, 1988), 195–210.
36. Reinhold Niebuhr, "Religion and Education," *Religious Education* 48 (November-December 1953): 373.

books, the Bible, and the most excellent of all persons, Jesus Christ. In fulfilling this duty we have an obligation to disclose the truth. All truth is God's truth, but not all truth is of the same order or on the same level.[37] The truth revealed in the person of Jesus Christ and the truths discerned in the Bible are those that hold priority in the dialogue within a pluralistic society. This stance celebrates the distinctives of Christian identity while maintaining an appropriate openness.

Christian identity is based upon ultimate foundations that cannot be compromised. In relation to these ultimate foundations, the words of C. S. Lewis are particularly instructive in a pluralistic society: "An open mind, in questions that are not ultimate, is useful. But an open mind about the ultimate foundations either of Theoretical or of practical Reason is idiocy."[38] The affirmation of foundations supports a Christian identity within a pluralistic society. Without such an identity openness is not a real possibility, for one then has little to share at the common table of dialogue. Sharing at a common table indicates the need for participation in the search for truth and in authoritative teaching. But before we consider participation, we must further explore the issues of identity and openness.

Tarasar's prescription of teaching for both identity and openness deserves careful study in the search for truth.[39] The stress upon identity is crucial in a pluralistic age. Persons need definition and boundaries to function in personal and communal life. The need for identity assumes some measure of exclusivity. The danger of this exclusivity is that it can lead to idolatry with one's or one's group identity being absolutized. We then are not open to strangers or to others who are also creatures of God and worthy of respect and care. The stress upon openness is also crucial in a pluralistic age. Persons need dialogue and interaction with a wide diversity of others who they may encounter each day. The need for openness assumes some measure of inclusivity. The dan-

---

37. Frank E. Gaebelein, *The Christian, the Arts, and Truth: Regaining the vision of Greatness*, ed. Bruce Lockerbie (Portland, Ore.: Multnomah, 1985), 144–45.

38. C. S. Lewis, *The Abolition of Man* (New York: Macmillan, 1947), 60.

39. Tarasar, "Minority Problem," 195.

ger of this inclusivity is that it can lead to relativism with its lack of norms, foundations, and organizing principles for life.

It is not strange to find the need for both exclusivity and inclusivity in education; these two themes are sounded by Jesus. As Jesus interacts with the Pharisees who opposed his work of healing, the Gospel writer records these words: "Whoever is not with me is against me, and whoever does not gather with me scatters" (Matt. 12:30; Luke 11:23). In his ministry Jesus set boundaries in terms of loyalty and commitment that are exclusive and demanding. Yet on another occasion, when the disciples encountered someone casting out demons in Jesus' name, they tried to stop him because he was not following them. Jesus' recorded response is a striking contrast to the other incident:

> "Do not stop him; for no one who does a deed of power in my name will be able soon afterward to speak evil of me. Whoever is not against us is for us. For truly I tell you, whoever gives you a cup of water to drink because you bear the name of Christ will by no means lose the reward." [Mark 9:39-41]

The Christian gospel embraces both elements of exclusivity that affirm identity and elements of inclusivity that affirm openness. Both elements are essential in authoritative teaching that wrestles with the truth in a pluralistic age. Authoritative teaching also requires a concern for participation in the faith community.

Participation

The World Council study identified a trend in many churches: for more people to participate in decision-making processes. It is interesting to note that one of the megatrends identified by the futurologist John Naisbitt is the movement from representative democracy to participatory democracy.[40] The principle of participatory democracy affirms that persons are to be a part of the decision-making process that affects their lives. In other words, persons have a right to share their perspectives and concerns on issues whose resolutions will affect them or involve their cooper-

40. John Naisbitt, *Megatrends: Ten Directions Transforming Our Lives* (New York: Warner, 1982).

140

ation and activity. The implication of such a principle is that the extent of participation in decision-making affects the level of ownership of decisions and their implementation.

The Council study theologically legitimated such participation on the basis that the gift of the Spirit is given to the whole church and that the discernment of truth needs to take place through the interaction among all of its members.[41] First, the emphasis on participation has implications for general education. This emphasis implies that students should be actively included in decisions that teachers make both in and outside of the classroom or the educational event. Such an emphasis has been advocated in self-directed andragogical teaching models that promote a move from teacher-directed to student-directed classroom strategies.[42] Second, administrators and policymakers in the field of education have been impressed with the need to involve teachers, parents, students, and various other constituencies that have an interest in education. This increased participation by various groups and persons involves a greater commitment to consultation and collaboration whenever they can be secured by leaders. Third, participation also involves the increased use of consensus decision-making strategies.

In addition to the impact of participation on general education, influences can be named in relation to Christian education. Participation can be encouraged because it results in increased learning and ownership of the educational process, but certain essentials or nonnegotiables exist in Christian education. For example, the lordship of Jesus Christ is affirmed as essential in Christian education, and the goal is for persons to own and live out this affirmation and to participate in decisions that seek to incarnate Christ's lordship in corporate and personal life. But the lordship of Christ and the demands of following him are not diminished by the lack of participation, nor are they revised by the proposals that emerge from active participation of persons who

41. "How Does the Church Teach Authoritatively Today?" 88.
42. For a discussion of andragogy, the art and science of facilitating the learning of adults, see Robert W. Pazmiño, "Adult Education with Persons from Ethnic Minority Communities," in *Christian Educator's Handbook on Adult Education*, ed. James C. Wilhoit and Kenneth O. Gangel (Wheaton: Victor, 1993).

suggest some such revision. The model of partnership encourages increased participation to enable interdependence and mutuality to emerge through Christian education (chap. 2).

Other observations in this area are warranted. First, certain decisions, given their personal and critical nature, cannot be subjected to the scrutiny of wide and varied participation. Second, the principle of participation raises serious questions about authoritarian educational approaches and educational decision-making. These questions do not diminish the appropriate place of authority in Christian education. The ultimate or fontal authority for Christian education is God, and human participation does not limit but enhances that authority as persons search for truth in community with God and others. That search requires an openness to and a reception of the truth.

Reception

The fourth and final aspect named in the World Council study was reception. A stronger emphasis on the need for reception of teaching by the whole church was noted. Reception was viewed as another aspect of participation, but one requiring special emphasis. "To the degree in which teaching has been arrived at through participation of the entire body of Christ, reception will be facilitated. Structures of participation at all levels of the Church prepare the way of reception."[43]

The study went on to define reception. Reception does not imply that decisions are arranged from above and then submitted to the community for passive acceptance. Reception involves not only formal endorsement, but also a profound appropriation through a gradual testing process "by which the teaching is digested into the life and liturgy of the community."[44] The Council study made the following observations that also serve to bring closure to this work:

> Ultimately, authoritative teaching is always an "event" which happens and cannot be organized or programmed, juridically or structurally. The authority of the Church is based on the author-

43. "How Does Church Teach Authoritatively?" 88.
44. Ibid.

ity of God and his design for the world in Jesus Christ; it depends on the gift of the Spirit. The teaching of Jesus was authenticated by his deeds and miracles. So, too, the Church's teaching will be authenticated by the blessings of the Spirit, not by "persuasive words of wisdom, but the manifestation of Spirit and power."[45]

The Spirit of God is identified in the Scriptures as the Spirit of truth. Those who teach and learn must be sensitive and open to the gentle promptings of the Spirit in their search for the truth. The challenge in a pluralistic age is to teach with both a liberating spirit and in communion with the liberating Spirit of God. The challenge for Christians today as through the ages is to teach with authority that is authenticated through their lives and actions. In this the truth will be shared.

Conclusion

This work has sought to answer the question By what authority do we teach? The question of authority is a crucial one for the Christian church to grapple with in responding to contemporary challenges. The answer to this question is suggested in how the question itself is posed. The inclusion of *we* rather than just *I* suggests that Christians must be in partnership with God (Father, Son, and Spirit), the Christian community, and others if authoritative and transformative teaching is to be practiced. The others include a host that embrace the Christian faith within a variety of traditions. They also include persons who embrace various world religions and secular faiths. But the distinctive authority for Christian teachers lies in their identity as Christians called and equipped by God for service and ministry. The final, ultimate, and fontal authority belongs to God revealed most wonderfully in Jesus Christ, the master teacher.

Ultimately the question By what authority do we teach? for the Christian teacher becomes by whose authority do we teach? The foundational and challenging answer to this question is that we teach by God's authority. This is both the privilege and the responsibility of Christian teaching in an age of pluralism. We

45. Ibid.

143

teach by the authority of God's call, enablement, enjoyment, and love. Many years ago the Christian teacher Augustine observed that "one loving spirit sets another spirit on fire." It is this teaching that holds the potential of being transformative.

Review

Chapter 1 of this work stressed the authority of God and God's call in answering the question By whose authority do we teach? God uses available human vessels to continue the ministry of teaching begun at creation and reaffirmed in the new creation made possible in Jesus Christ. Christian teachers teach at the bidding or the call of God and as commissioned by the resurrected Christ (Matt. 28:18–20). Christian teachers teach by the power and enablement of God through the ministry of the Holy Spirit. This is a high calling and worth the best efforts of the whole people of God.

Chapter 2 explored the context in which authoritative teaching is exercised and without which it cannot properly function. The Christian church, the faith community, provides the ethos and the structure within which Christian teachers serve others and fulfill God's intentions for teaching the Christian faith. The Christian church is understood in both its gathered and scattered expressions; in it Christians serve in a wide variety of settings. The unity amid the diversity of service is found in God's mission and its inherent connected character that links proclamation, community formation, service, witness, advocacy, and worship. Given the corporate character of Christian teaching, the model advocated to guide teachers is partnership with God and others.

Chapter 3 considered the question of the authority of one's person and gifts. This personally appropriated authority for teaching was analyzed in terms of the distinctives of Christian spirituality and the examples of the *anawim*. Giftedness is directly related to one's availability to be used by God to meet the needs for teaching within the Christian community and the wider world. Giftedness is also related to one's willingness to become a disciple of Jesus throughout one's life and eternity. The

144

anawim were willing to risk all and rely upon the provision of God. Such is the need in Christian teaching that can be identified as anointed.

The focus of chapter 4 was upon the authority of experience, in particular the experience of God. This experience of God is by the grace of God and through the exercise of faith (Eph. 2:8–9). Experience brings life to the content of Christian teaching. But in an age of uninformed and unexamined experience, discernment is required. Guidelines for the discernment of experience were suggested: consultation with Scripture and the wider faith community down through the ages and in present times. In order to teach with authority, Christian teachers must pay attention to the intersection of their faith experiences of feeling, thought, and commitment.

Chapter 5 explored the authority of one's expertise and study. For the Christian teacher this implies the proper use of reason and reflection in the service of the faith. The goal of such effort is to acquire the mind of Christ so as to better love God with all one's mind. This is a lifelong task requiring discipline and dialogue with a wide variety of other persons who also seek to discern God's truth for our time. Such is required of Christian teachers who must move beyond a milk diet. Maturity of thought is required in order to consume and share the solid food of God's Word (Heb. 5:12–14) with persons who desperately need spiritual nourishment.

The final chapter wrestled with a task that is before Christian teachers at the beginning of the third millennium. That task is both to affirm one's Christian identity and to enter a wider dialogue in a religiously pluralistic world. This dialogue is a risk (see the description of "spoiling the Egyptians" in chapter 5). Not to be open to this wider discussion results in a cultural isolation and ghettoization that Christian teachers can ill afford. This chapter illustrated the insights gained from the author's direct experience with this wider dialogue.

A prayer that accompanies this work is that Christians will joyfully and discerningly teach with authority as we draw upon the sources available to us in God. This teaching will fulfill God's mission in the world. It will also model the partnership made possible in the Christian church through the ministry of the Holy Spirit. The Spirit seeks to empower Christian educators for their various teaching ministries and waits upon the availability of those called to teach. Those called are disciples of Jesus who are willing and gifted to disciple others through their teaching.

Select Bibliography

God's Authority

Blendinger, Christian. "Might, Authority, Throne." In *The New International Dictionary of New Testament Theology*, 3 vols., edited by Colin Brown, 2:601–16. Grand Rapids: Zondervan, 1976.

Bloesch, Donald G. *The Crisis of Piety: Essays Towards a Theology of the Christian Life*. Colorado Springs: Helmers and Howard, 1988.

Diehl, Judith Ruhe. *A Woman's Place: Equal Partnership in Daily Ministry*. Philadelphia: Fortress, 1985.

Fackre, Gabriel. J. *The Christian Story: A Pastoral Systematics*. Vol. 2, *Authority: Scripture in the Church for the World*. Grand Rapids: Eerdmans, 1987.

Ferré, Nels F. S. *A Theology for Christian Education*. Philadelphia, Westminster, 1967.

Forsyth, P. T. *The Gospel and Authority: A P. T. Forsyth Reader*. Edited by Marvin W. Anderson. Minneapolis: Augsburg, 1971.

———. *The Principle of Authority in Relation to Certainty, Sanctity and Society: An Essay in the Philosophy of Experiential Religion*. 2d ed. London: Independent, 1952.

Guthrie, Donald. "Jesus." In *A History of Religious Educators*, edited by Elmer L. Towns, 15–38. Grand Rapids: Baker, 1975.

Marsh, John. "Authority." In *The Interpreter's Dictionary of the Bible*, edited by George A. Buttrick, 319–20. Nashville: Abingdon, 1962.

Pazmiño, Robert W. *Foundational Issues in Christian Education: An Introduction in Evangelical Perspective*. Grand Rapids: Baker, 1988.

Russell, Letty M. "Authority in Mutual Ministry." *Quarterly Review* 6 (Spring 1986): 10–23.

Sennet, Richard. *Authority*. New York: Vintage, 1981.

Authority in the Church

Bauer, Arthur O. F. *Being in Mission: A Resource for the Local Church and Community.* New York: Friendship, 1987.

Bosch, David J. *Transforming Mission: Paradigm Shifts in Theology of Mission.* Maryknoll, N.Y.: Orbis, 1991.

Carroll, Jackson W. *As One with Authority: Reflective Leadership in Ministry.* Louisville: Westminster/John Knox, 1991.

————. "Some Issues in Clergy Authority." *Review of Religious Research* 23 (December 1981): 99–108.

Emler, Donald G. *Revisioning the DRE.* Birmingham, Ala.: Religious Education Press, 1989.

Gehris, Paul D., and Katherine A. Gehris. *The Teaching Church—Active in Mission.* Valley Forge, Penn.: Judson, 1987.

Messer, Donald E. *A Conspiracy of Goodness: Contemporary Images of Christian Mission.* Nashville: Abingdon, 1992.

Osmer, Richard R. *A Teachable Spirit: Recovering the Teaching Office in the Church.* Louisville: Westminster/John Knox, 1990.

Pazmiño, Robert W. *Principles and Practices of Christian Education: An Evangelical Perspective.* Grand Rapids: Baker, 1992.

Russell, Letty M. *Household of Freedom: Authority in Feminist Theology.* Philadelphia: Fortress, 1987.

Person's Authority and Gifts

Bonhoeffer, Dietrich. *The Cost of Discipleship.* Rev ed. New York: Macmillan, 1979.

González, Justo L. *Mañana: Christian Theology from a Hispanic Perspective.* Nashville: Abingdon, 1990.

Habermas, Ronald, and Klaus Issler. *Teaching for Reconciliation: Foundations and Practice of Christian Education Ministry.* Grand Rapids: Baker, 1992.

Harper, Norman E. *Making Disciples: The Challenge of Christian Education at the End of the 20th Century.* Memphis: Christian Studies Center, 1981.

Pazmiño, Robert W. "Nurturing the Spiritual Life of Teachers." In *Christian Educator's Handbook on Spiritual Formation*, edited by Kenneth O. Gangel and James C. Wilhoit. Wheaton: Victor, 1994.

Sawicki, Marianne. *The Gospel in History: Portrait of a Teaching Church: The Origins of Christian Education.* New York: Paulist, 1988.

Spiritual Formation in Theological Education: An Invitation to Partici-pate. Geneva: Programme on Theological Education, World Council of Churches, 1987.

Authority of Experience

Boys, Mary C. *Educating in Faith: Maps and Visions*. San Francisco: Harper and Row, 1989.

Cram, Ronald H. "Christian Education in Theological Education." *Religious Education* 87 (Summer 1992): 331–36.

Freire, Paulo. *Pedagogy of the Oppressed*. Translated by Myra Bergman Ramos. New York: Seabury, 1970.

Gillespie, V. Bailey. *The Experience of Faith*. Birmingham, Ala.: Religious Education Press, 1988.

Groome, Thomas H. *Sharing Faith: A Comprehensive Approach to Religious Education and Pastoral Ministry: The Way of Shared Praxis*. San Francisco: Harper San Francisco, 1991.

Johnson, Susanne. *Christian Spiritual Formation in the Church and Classroom*. Nashville: Abingdon, 1989.

LeBar, Lois E. "Curriculum." In *An Introduction to Evangelical Christian Education*, edited by J. Edward Hakes, 86–95. Chicago: Moody, 1964.

Solivan, Samuel. "Orthopathos: Interlocutor between Orthodoxy and Praxis." *Andover Newton Review* 1 (Winter 1990): 19–25.

Steele, Les L. *On the Way: A Practical Theology of Christian Formation*. Grand Rapids: Baker, 1990.

Westerhoff, John II. III. *Bringing Up Children in the Christian Faith*. Minneapolis: Winston, 1980.

———. *Will Our Children Have Faith?* New York: Seabury, 1976.

Authority of Expertise and Study

Carroll, Jackson W. *As One with Authority: Reflective Leadership in Ministry*. Louisville: Westminster/John Knox, 1991.

Cremin, Lawrence A. *Public Education*. New York: Basic, 1976.

Gaebelein, Frank E. *The Christian, the Arts, and the Truth: Regaining the Vision of Greatness*, edited by Bruce Lockerbie. Portland, Ore.: Multnomah, 1985.

Gariboldi, Ronald, and Daniel Novotny. *The Art of Theological Reflection: An Ecumenical Study*, edited by Jean S. Novotny. Lanham, Md.: University Press of America, 1987.

Palmer, Parker J. *To Know As We Are Known: A Spirituality of Education*. San Francisco: Harper and Row, 1983.

Sholl, Doug. "Unity and Uniqueness: A Theology of Christian Relationships." In *Moral Development Foundations: Judeo-Christian Alternatives to Piaget/Kohlberg,* edited by Donald M. Joy. Nashville: Abingdon, 1983, 183–206.

Smith, Huston. "Excluded Knowledge: A Critique of the Modern Mind Set." *Teachers College Record* (February 1979): 419–45.

Whitehead, Evelyn E., and James D. Whitehead. *Method in Ministry: Theological Reflection and Christian Ministry.* San Francisco: Harper and Row, 1980.

Wolterstorff, Nicholas P. *Educating for Responsible Action.* Grand Rapids: Eerdmans, 1980.

———. *Reason Within the Bounds of Religion.* 2d ed. Grand Rapids: Eerdmans, 1984.

Wrobbel, Karen A. "Teaching for Thinking: A Must for Christian Education." *Christian Education Journal* 12 (Spring 1992): 149–50.

Authority in Age of Pluralism

Banks, James A. *Multiethnic Education: Theory and Practice.* 2d ed. Boston: Allyn and Bacon, 1988.

Faith and Order Commission. "How Does the Church Teach Authoritatively Today?: Faith and Order Paper No. 91." *The Ecumenical Review* 31 (January 1979): 77–93.

Foster, Charles R., ed. *Ethnicity in the Education of the Church.* Nashville: Scarritt, 1987.

Garcia, Ricardo L. *Teaching in a Pluralistic Society: Concepts, Models and Strategies.* New York: Harper and Row, 1982.

Gross, Victor. *Educating to Reverence: The Legacy of Abraham Heschel.* Bristol, Ind.: Wyndham Hall, 1989.

Lewis, C. S. *The Abolition of Man.* New York: Macmillan, 1947.

Pazmiño, Robert W. "Adult Education with Persons from Ethnic Minority Communities." In *Christian Educator's Handbook on Adult Education,* edited by James C. Wilhoit and Kenneth O. Gangel, 278–88. Wheaton: Victor, 1993.

———. "Double Dutch: Reflections of an Hispanic North American on Multicultural Religious Education," In *Voces: Voices from the Hispanic Church,* edited by Justo L. González, 137–45. Nashville: Abingdon, 1992.

———. *Latin American Journey: Insights for Christian Education in North America.* Cleveland: United Church Press, 1994.

Thompson, Norma H. *Religious Pluralism and Religious Education.* Birmingham, Ala.: Religious Education Press, 1988.

Index of Subjects